# SOCIAL STUDIES: STANDARDS, MEANING, AND UNDERSTANDING

Barbara Slater Stern

EYE ON EDUCATION

EYE ON EDUCATION
6 DEPOT WAY WEST, SUITE 106
LARCHMONT, NY 10538
(914) 833–0551
(914) 833–0761 fax
www.eyeoneducation.com

Copyright © 2002 Eye On Education, Inc.
All Rights Reserved.

For information about permission to reproduce selections from this book, write: Eye On Education, Permissions Dept., Suite 106, 6 Depot Way West, Larchmont, NY 10538.

**Library of Congress Cataloging-in-Publication Data**

Stern, Barbara Slater, 1949-
  Social studies : standards, meaning, and understanding / Barbara Slater Stern.
       p. cm.
  Includes bibliographical references.
  ISBN 1-930556-30-6
    1. Social sciences--Study and teaching. I. Title.

H62 .S7543 2002
300'.71'2--dc21                                              2002019851

10 9 8 7 6 5 4 3 2 1

Editorial and production services provided by
Richard H. Adin Freelance Editorial Services
52 Oakwood Blvd., Poughkeepsie, NY 12603-4112
(845-471-3566)

## Also Available from EYE ON EDUCATION

**DIFFERENTIATED INSTRUCTION:
A GUIDE FOR MIDDLE AND HIGH SCHOOL TEACHERS**
Amy Benjamin

**COACHING AND MENTORING
FIRST YEAR AND STUDENT TEACHERS**
India Podsen and Vicki Denmark

**CONSTRUCTIVIST STRATEGIES: MEETING STANDARDS
AND ENGAGING ADOLESCENT MINDS**
Foote, Vermette and Battaglia

**PERFORMANCE STANDARDS AND AUTHENTIC LEARNING**
Allan Glatthorn

**WRITING IN THE CONTENT AREAS**
Amy Benjamin

**THE PAIDEIA CLASSROOM:
TEACHING FOR UNDERSTANDING**
Terry Roberts with Laura Billings

**PERSONALIZED INSTRUCTION**
James Keefe and John Jenkins

**COLLABORATIVE LEARNING IN MIDDLE AND SECONDARY
SCHOOLS: APPLICATIONS AND ASSESSMENTS**
Dawn Snodgrass and Mary Bevevino

**RESEARCH ON EDUCATIONAL INNOVATIONS 3/E**
Arthur K. Ellis

**TRANSFORMING SCHOOLS INTO COMMUNITY
LEARNING CENTERS**
Steve Parson

**ENCOURAGING STUDENT ENGAGEMENT
IN THE BLOCK**
David Marshak

**TEACHING IN THE BLOCK**
Robert Lynn Canady and Michael Rettig

**SOCRATIC SEMINARS IN THE BLOCK**
Wanda Ball and Pam Brewer

DEDICATION

For Mark, Jeff, and Ben.

# Table of Contents

Preface . . . . . . . . . . . . . . . . . . . . . . . . . . . . . . . . . . . . . . . xi

About the Author . . . . . . . . . . . . . . . . . . . . . . . . . . . . . . xiv

**1 Introducing Curriculum Alignment** . . . . . . . . . . . . . . . . . . 1
   Definition of Authentic Instruction . . . . . . . . . . . . . . . . . . . 2
      Constructing Meaning. . . . . . . . . . . . . . . . . . . . . . . . . . 2
      Using Disciplined Inquiry to Construct Meaning. . . . . . . . . . . . . 4
      Value or Meaning Beyond Success in School . . . . . . . . . . 4
      Producing Knowledge. . . . . . . . . . . . . . . . . . . . . . . . . 4
   Criteria for Authentic Assessment . . . . . . . . . . . . . . . . . . . . . 5
      Higher-Order Thinking . . . . . . . . . . . . . . . . . . . . . . . 6
      Depth of Knowledge. . . . . . . . . . . . . . . . . . . . . . . . . 6
      Connectedness to the Real World. . . . . . . . . . . . . . . . . . 7
      Substantive Conversation. . . . . . . . . . . . . . . . . . . . . . 8
      Social Support . . . . . . . . . . . . . . . . . . . . . . . . . . . 8
   Other Views of Authentic Instruction and Assessment . . . . . . . . . . 9
      An Interdisciplinary Approach . . . . . . . . . . . . . . . . . . . 9
      Standards: National, State, and Local . . . . . . . . . . . . . . . 10
      Technology . . . . . . . . . . . . . . . . . . . . . . . . . . . . 10
      Putting It All Together . . . . . . . . . . . . . . . . . . . . . . 11

**2 Authentic Tasks and Rubrics** . . . . . . . . . . . . . . . . . . . . 13
   The Limits of Traditional Assessment . . . . . . . . . . . . . . . . . 13
   The Benefits of Authentic, Performance-Based Assessment. . . . . . . . 14
   Reaching Out to Others . . . . . . . . . . . . . . . . . . . . . . . 15
   Understanding Curriculum Alignment . . . . . . . . . . . . . . . . . 17
   Designing Authentic Performance Tasks and Assessments . . . . . . . 18
   Designing Evaluation Rubrics. . . . . . . . . . . . . . . . . . . . . 21
   Communicating with Students and Parents about Grades . . . . . . . 23
   Conclusion . . . . . . . . . . . . . . . . . . . . . . . . . . . . . 24

**3 Integrating Performance Tasks and Rubrics: FAQ's** . . . . . . . . 27
   Will I Be Changing My Whole Course? . . . . . . . . . . . . . . . . 27
   Will This Be Too Much Work
      Given All My Other Teacher Duties?. . . . . . . . . . . . . . . 28
   Will the Students Want to Work This Hard? . . . . . . . . . . . . . 28
   We Have Standardized State Exams. How Can I Find
      Time for These Projects? . . . . . . . . . . . . . . . . . . . . 29

How Can I Be Sure My Students Are Really Learning the
    Content if I Don't Lecture and Assign Worksheets or
    Chapter Questions?. . . . . . . . . . . . . . . . . . . . . . . . . . . . 30
How Do I Adapt the Lessons/Units I Am Currently Using? . . . . . . . 31
I Am Still Worried about My Students' Willingness to
    Do This Much Work . . . . . . . . . . . . . . . . . . . . . . . . . . 32
My Technology Skills Are Weak. How Will I Integrate
    Technology into the Lessons?. . . . . . . . . . . . . . . . . . . . . 32
How Will My Special Needs Students Complete These Projects?. . . . . 33
How Can I Be Confident That My
    Grading Is Fair (Valid and Reliable)?. . . . . . . . . . . . . . . . . 33

# 4  Social Studies Themes . . . . . . . . . . . . . . . . . . . . . 37

## Culture . . . . . . . . . . . . . . . . . . . . . . . . . . . . . . . 39
The Regional Differences in American History . . . . . . . . . . . . . . 42
Evaluation Rubric . . . . . . . . . . . . . . . . . . . . . . . . . . . . . 47
Coping with Change: The Rise of Modern Europe . . . . . . . . . . . . 48
Student Self Evaluation Form . . . . . . . . . . . . . . . . . . . . . . . 53
Presentation Evaluation . . . . . . . . . . . . . . . . . . . . . . . . . . 53
Group Evaluation Form . . . . . . . . . . . . . . . . . . . . . . . . . . 54
Evaluation Rubric . . . . . . . . . . . . . . . . . . . . . . . . . . . . . 55

## Time, Continuity, and Change . . . . . . . . . . . . . . . . . 56
Understanding Maps. . . . . . . . . . . . . . . . . . . . . . . . . . . . 58
Assignment Sheet: The Ancient World or Medieval World . . . . . . . . 61
Evaluation Rubric . . . . . . . . . . . . . . . . . . . . . . . . . . . . . 63
What Would Life Be Like If? . . . . . . . . . . . . . . . . . . . . . . . 64
Evaluation Rubric . . . . . . . . . . . . . . . . . . . . . . . . . . . . . 66

## People, Places, and Environments . . . . . . . . . . . . . . . 68
Sports Vacation Regional Geography . . . . . . . . . . . . . . . . . . . 70
Evaluation Rubric . . . . . . . . . . . . . . . . . . . . . . . . . . . . . 73
Example of a Benchmark for This Lesson . . . . . . . . . . . . . . . . . 74
Why Are Things Where They Are?. . . . . . . . . . . . . . . . . . . . . 75
Evaluation Rubric . . . . . . . . . . . . . . . . . . . . . . . . . . . . . 79

## Individual Development and Identity. . . . . . . . . . . . . . 81
Person of the Year . . . . . . . . . . . . . . . . . . . . . . . . . . . . 83
Evaluation Rubric . . . . . . . . . . . . . . . . . . . . . . . . . . . . . 87
Why Did You Do That? . . . . . . . . . . . . . . . . . . . . . . . . . . 88
Evaluation Rubric . . . . . . . . . . . . . . . . . . . . . . . . . . . . . 93
Scored Discussions . . . . . . . . . . . . . . . . . . . . . . . . . . . . 95
Scored Discussion Checklist. . . . . . . . . . . . . . . . . . . . . . . . 97

## Individuals, Groups, and Institutions . . . . . . . . . . . . . 99
Child Labor: Yesterday and Today . . . . . . . . . . . . . . . . . . . 100

Declaration of Dependence by the Children of America in
  Mines and Factories and Workshops Assembled . . . . . . . . . . . 103
Questions for Students from Text Set Article Read . . . . . . . . . . 104
Text Set. . . . . . . . . . . . . . . . . . . . . . . . . . . . . . . . . . . . . . . . . 105
Readers Theater Example . . . . . . . . . . . . . . . . . . . . . . . . . . 108
Politics and Religion . . . . . . . . . . . . . . . . . . . . . . . . . . . . . . 111
Scored Discussion Checklist . . . . . . . . . . . . . . . . . . . . . . . . 119

**Power, Authority, and Governance** . . . . . . . . . . . . . . . . . . . **121**
What Are My Rights?. . . . . . . . . . . . . . . . . . . . . . . . . . . . . 122
Evaluation Rubric. . . . . . . . . . . . . . . . . . . . . . . . . . . . . . . . 125
The Government and the World Wide Web . . . . . . . . . . . . 127
Evaluation Rubric. . . . . . . . . . . . . . . . . . . . . . . . . . . . . . . . 131

**Production, Distribution, and Consumption** . . . . . . . . . . . . **132**
But, I Love My Nikes . . . . . . . . . . . . . . . . . . . . . . . . . . . . . 133
Evaluation Rubric. . . . . . . . . . . . . . . . . . . . . . . . . . . . . . . . 138
My Paycheck Shrunk!. . . . . . . . . . . . . . . . . . . . . . . . . . . . . 141
Evaluation Rubric. . . . . . . . . . . . . . . . . . . . . . . . . . . . . . . . 146

**Science, Technology, and Society** . . . . . . . . . . . . . . . . . . . . **147**
The Technology of Warfare . . . . . . . . . . . . . . . . . . . . . . . . 149
Evaluation Rubric. . . . . . . . . . . . . . . . . . . . . . . . . . . . . . . . 153
Epidemics Then and Now: The Plague and AIDS. . . . . . . . . 154
Evaluation Rubric. . . . . . . . . . . . . . . . . . . . . . . . . . . . . . . . 158

**Global Connections** . . . . . . . . . . . . . . . . . . . . . . . . . . . . . . **159**
Reviewing World History Concepts . . . . . . . . . . . . . . . . . . 160
Current Events/Classifying Information. . . . . . . . . . . . . . . . 161
Evaluation Rubric. . . . . . . . . . . . . . . . . . . . . . . . . . . . . . . . 164
A Global Village? . . . . . . . . . . . . . . . . . . . . . . . . . . . . . . . . 165
Evaluation Rubric. . . . . . . . . . . . . . . . . . . . . . . . . . . . . . . . 169

**Civic Ideals and Practices.** . . . . . . . . . . . . . . . . . . . . . . . . . **170**
Unfair? . . . . . . . . . . . . . . . . . . . . . . . . . . . . . . . . . . . . . . . 172
Evaluation Rubric. . . . . . . . . . . . . . . . . . . . . . . . . . . . . . . . 176
More Than Two Political Parties? . . . . . . . . . . . . . . . . . . . . 177
Evaluation Rubric. . . . . . . . . . . . . . . . . . . . . . . . . . . . . . . . 181

# Conclusion . . . . . . . . . . . . . . . . . . . . . . . . . . . . . . . . . . . . . 183

# References . . . . . . . . . . . . . . . . . . . . . . . . . . . . . . . . . . . . . 185

# List of Lessons by Standard and Subject

◆ Lesson is focused on the subject
● Lesson can be modified for the subject
○ Lesson can be used for the subject with major changes

| Lesson Name | Lesson Topic | World History | US History | Geography | Economics | Civics/Government |
|---|---|---|---|---|---|---|
| **NCSS Standard: Culture** | | | | | | |
| Regional Differences | American colonization and settlement pre-revolution | | ◆ | | | |
| Coping with Change: the Rise of Modern Europe | Rise of the early modern European monarchies | ◆ | | ○ | | |
| **NCSS Standard: Time, Continuity and Change** | | | | | | |
| Understanding Maps | Influence of geography on world history (mapping project) | ◆ | ○ | ◆ | | |
| What Would It Be Like If? | Questions about how life would be in a different place or time | ◆ | ◆ | ◆ | ◆ | |
| **NCSS Standard: People, Places, and Environments** | | | | | | |
| Why Are Things Where They Are? | Theories of Urban Place Location | ○ | ◆ | ◆ | | |
| Sports Vacation Regional Geography | Plan a trip | ○ | ○ | ◆ | ○ | |
| **NCSS Standard: Individual Development and Identity** | | | | | | |
| Person of the Year | Nominate and select a famous leader | ◆ | ◆ | | | ○ (restrict to a political leader) |
| Why Did You Do That? | Historical Empathy; Holocaust | ◆ | ◆ | | | |

# List of Lessons by Standard and Subject

| Lesson Name | Lesson Topic | World History | US History | Geography | Economics | Civics/Government |
|---|---|---|---|---|---|---|
| **NCSS Standard: Individuals, Groups, and Institutions** | | | | | | |
| Child Labor: Yesterday and Today | U.S. History: Lewis Hines Pictures | ◆ | ◆ | | ○ | |
| Politics and Religion | Rise and Spread of Islam | ◆ | | | | |
| **NCSS Standard: Power, Authority, and Governance** | | | | | | |
| What are My Rights? | Bill of Rights and School Discipline Code | ◆ | | | | ◆ |
| Government and The World Wide Web | Censorship policies of World Governments | ◆ | ◆ | | | ◆ |
| **NCSS Standard: Production, Distribution, and Consumption** | | | | | | |
| But, I Love My Nikes | Global economy | ○ | ○ | | ◆ | |
| My Paycheck Shrunk | Taxation | ● (Social Security) | ● | ○ | | |
| **NCSS Standard: Science, Technology, and Society** | | | | | | |
| The Technology of Warfare | History of Weapons | ◆ | ○ | | | |
| Epidemics Then and Now | The Black Plague and AIDS or U.S. with Influenza and AIDS | ◆ | ◆ | | | |
| **NCSS Standard: Global Connections** | | | | | | |
| Reviewing World History Concepts | PERSIA and current events projects | ◆ | ○ | | | |
| A Global Village | World Treaties U.S. 20th Century | ◆ | ◆ | | | ● (foreign policy) |

| Lesson Name | Lesson Topic | World History | US History | Geo-graphy | Econom-ics | Civics/ Govern-ment |
|---|---|---|---|---|---|---|
| **NCSS Standard: Civic Ideals and Practices** | | | | | | |
| Unfair! | Jurisprudential approach, teenage driving | ◆ | | | | ◆ |
| More than Two Political Parties? | Third parties in U.S. | ○ (modify for par-liamen-tary sys-tem) | ◆ | | | ◆ |

# Preface

Everywhere I go, teachers relate stories of how stressful their jobs have become. Why would they need a book championing authentic learning and authentic assessment at a time when national and state standards movements have overwhelmingly focused on high-stakes multiple choice tests? Tests based on the memorization of what seems like an ever-increasing factual content base coupled with what feels like an ever-decreasing amount of time in which to teach it. The answer is not difficult if the needs of both the students and their teachers are considered.

Popular wisdom in the field of social studies/history reports that of all the subjects students are required to study in school, social studies is the most disliked. Every time I, as a social studies teacher and teacher educator, hear that, I feel like weeping. How can it be that the social studies, where we learn about who we are and how we came to be that way, as well as where we try to predict where we should be heading and why, is so hated by students?

Could it be that students do not really understand the goals and purposes of the discipline? Are they convinced that social studies is just about the memorization of copious amounts of unrelated content—facts and dates—that accumulate unceasingly? And, our present method of ensuring attainment of these facts, the omnipresent multiple-choice test, is increasingly becoming a more and more high-stakes endeavor for many students and their teachers. This reinforces student dislike of social studies as teachers spend more time than ever lecturing and drilling for these tests.

If our goal as social studies educators, as defined by the National Council for the Social Studies (NCSS), is to help prepare our students to become active participants in our democratic society, or good citizens, how does this memorization of the content help us attain that goal? As far back as 1949, Allan Griffin, a social studies educator, explained quite clearly that the causal link between the study of United States history with behavior defined as "good citizenship" could not be made. His point was that the acquisition of knowledge, the knowing "that" or "what" does not appear to have much relationship to the utilization of that knowledge. More importantly, current research in learning theory holds that if academic content has meaning to students, then they will be able to learn it more easily and to retain that knowledge for longer periods of time. Thus, a case is made that traditional lecture and memorization will not necessarily yield either higher test scores or good citizenship.

What becomes obvious is that social studies classes and teachers must strive toward curriculum and assessment that enable students to create meaning.

Thus, the belief by many teachers that authentic learning and authentic assessment will not yield the necessary test scores is unfounded. If students are motivated by, and interested in, their task, that is, if they enjoy social studies/history class, the content base can be mastered along the way. Then their test scores would increase along with their ability to utilize the knowledge acquired to become active, participating citizens in our country and the world. We can, to quote the old adage, "kill two birds with one stone."

The purposes of this book are first, to introduce secondary social studies teachers to the goals and objectives of authentic learning and authentic assessment. Second, to demonstrate to teachers how to plan their curriculum and lessons around authentic assignments while taking into consideration curriculum standards and tests now in place in many states and school districts. Third, to provide examples of authentic instruction across the social studies disciplines and secondary grade levels in order to give teachers a beginning toward implementing authentic instruction in their classrooms. Fourth, to provide multiple examples utilizing technology, particularly Web-based technology, to enable teachers to integrate technology skills and resources with social studies content effectively.

The first three chapters address goals one and two. These chapters define authentic instruction and build the case for adapting social studies curriculum to a more student-centered, interactive classroom environment. The second part of the book addresses goals three and four. It consists of an introduction, Chapter 4, and the following ten sections provide lesson plan examples of authentic instruction and, frequently, the integration of technology.

Each section in Chapter 4 is related to a theme or strand of the National Council of the Social Studies standards, *Expectations of Excellence* (1994). There are two lesson plans for each theme. The lesson plans are also linked to the national standards in the various social studies subject areas: world history, U.S. history, geography, economics, and civics/government. Each lesson can be adapted for other social studies subjects.

One note about technology integration is in order. For lessons that are technology based, either the section introduction or the lesson plan itself provides ideas for teachers who either do not have the necessary technology equipment or the technical know-how. Web-based lessons are the most frequent as that seems to be the way the education curriculum is developing. Web-based lessons do not become old as quickly as software-based lessons because the Web is more easily updated. Web-based lessons also prevent schools from having to make large capital outlays for software that will need upgrading every other year.

The introductions for each of the sections in Chapter 4 suggest ways for teachers to adapt the lessons for use in multiple social studies areas. In addition, the introductions to the sections provide ideas for interdisciplinary or multidisciplinary curriculum integration with the lessons. For interdisciplinary teaching, the lesson provides an opportunity for teachers to see places in their curriculum where they could work with colleagues by co-teaching a topic in more than one class. Although traditionally that class is English, suggestions for team teaching with math, business, or science are included.

# Preface

If that planning is too hard to arrange, the theme or main concept of the lesson could be taught in more than one class at different times with different uses. This multidisciplinary approach enables teachers to develop an idea across subjects without having to coordinate quite so carefully with others. If this is not feasible in your school, given that the lessons often use cooperative learning, sometimes a multidisciplinary approach can be developed within the classroom.

It is my hope that you will read the first three chapters of this book to develop an understanding of authentic instruction. After that, I hope that you will use the lesson plans to begin to change your instructional strategies. This change can be as gradual or rapid as you and your students are comfortable with. Feel free to modify the lessons to meet your needs. Over time, I hope you will develop the confidence to design your own lessons that incorporate authentic learning and authentic assessment. The task in the beginning may be time-consuming and, sometimes, frustrating. As your students begin to enjoy social studies class more, I hope you find your original investment in trying out these new strategies beneficial.

Finally, I would like to acknowledge several individuals who have assisted me and provided support as this book was completed. The School of Education at James Madison University provided me with course release to give me time to write the original manuscript. Ruth Crowell from Lyman High School, Longwood, Florida, read early versions of the first chapters and encouraged me to complete the book. The former students in my world history and A.P. U.S. history classes at Lyman High School served as the testing ground for several of these lessons. These students helped me learn much of what I know about the teaching of social studies.

My son, Jeff Mandell, and Karen Monger helped edit the first draft of the manuscript and gave me several useful ideas for simplifying the text. Mary Pontillo, the Secondary Education Program graduate assistant at James Madison University, assisted with editing. Additionally, Karen Harvey assisted with final editing. Several former JMU students, now teachers, have contributed lesson ideas that are credited to them on the lessons. John Rossi, Virginia Commonwealth University and Tom Mix, Murray High School, Charlottesville, Virginia, shared their rubric for scored discussions. Lastly, my husband, Mark Stern, provided emotional support as I struggled with writing this book. He always believes that I can do whatever I set out to do. That steadfast belief sees me through whenever I hit a tough spot on the road to completing a task.

# About the Author

Barbara Slater Stern has taught a variety of social studies courses at the high school level including United States History, World History, European Culture Studies, African-American History, and A.P. U.S. History. She has been an A.P. Reader for the U.S. History exam. She is an active member of the National Council for the Social Studies (NCSS) and has presented in-service and staff development sessions at NCSS, the Virginia Council of the Social Studies and the James Madison University Summer Standards of Learning Content Academy. She served on the ISTE NETS2 writing team focusing on integrating technology into social studies lessons and has presented a workshop for NCSS at the National Education Computing Conference (NECC). She has served on the NCSS Research and Instruction committees. She has a B.A. from the University of Rhode Island in Social Sciences and Secondary Education, an M.A. from the University of Louisville in Higher Education, and an Ed.D. in Curriculum and Instruction from the University of Central Florida. She is currently an associate professor at James Madison University in the Secondary Education Program where she teachers Methods of Teaching Social Studies in Secondary Schools, Curriculum and Foundations of Education courses.

# 1
# Introducing Curriculum Alignment

The current research on effective teaching calls for curriculum alignment. Curriculum alignment can be explained as: stating your objectives, teaching to your objectives, and testing those same objectives. The idea is that if you and your students are clear about where you are headed, you head there, and then, you check to see you are actually there, the desired learning will occur. In this age of standards and high-stakes, end-of-course testing, the need for curriculum alignment is clear. But, how can teachers take required curriculum and make it meaningful and important to students so that they actually learn it? The answer can be found in authentic instruction.

Authentic instruction can be pictured as an umbrella term that encompasses two sections: authentic learning and authentic assessment (see Figure 1.1). To borrow from the Chinese Yin/Yang symbol, envision authentic instruction as the large circle with authentic learning and authentic assessment as the two components that make it complete.

### Figure 1.1. Authentic Instruction

This suggests that as we plan lessons, we envision each unit of curriculum that we teach as a complete circle. This means that we consider the learning phase and the testing phase simultaneously. During the class period, teachers frequently are bombarded by students asking: "Do we have to know this? Is this important? Will it be on the test?" Combining the instruction and the assessment phases of teaching during unit and lesson planning ensures that teachers are able to answer these questions confidently.

As Figure 1.1 illustrates, authentic instruction takes the assessment component into the forefront of lesson planning because the students are informed at the start of the unit or lesson what product they will be responsible for at the end of the learning cycle. This works quite well in accountability settings. Although some school systems have not yet moved to high-stakes, end-of-course tests, they still may require teachers to demonstrate learning outcomes on their lesson plans. In other words, administrators and the public want teachers to be able to prove that students have actually mastered the material being taught; they want accountability.

For example, the effective teaching literature reminds teachers not to fall into the habit of closing class by saying, "O.K. class today we have learned…" because although you know what you tried to teach, the only way you know for sure what students learned is to ask them. To be truly accountable, the teacher must have the students demonstrate their learning as an outcome of the lesson in some concrete manner, thereby proving that the desired learning has occurred.

Where authentic instruction differs from traditional instruction is that both the learning and the assessment phase require more than academic content regurgitation. Using the tools of the discipline, the students must produce and use their new knowledge in a way that demonstrates that they understand the meaning and/or purpose of what has been taught. How is this accomplished?

## Definition of Authentic Instruction

In the traditional view of instruction, the teacher is the teller or the transmitter of information and the student is the passive learner of that information. Authentic instruction reverses the process and views the student as the active participant and the teacher as a facilitator or a guide. Newmann and Wehlage (1993) define authentic instruction as achievement that is significant and meaningful based upon students':

- Constructing meaning and producing knowledge;
- Using disciplined inquiry to construct meaning; and
- Aiming their work toward production or performance that has value or meaning beyond success in school (high grades).

This requires students to use the academic content of social studies (facts and concepts) and the tools (skills and methods) of social scientists to create a performance or product that will be useful to the student beyond the walls of the classroom. Thus, the assessment moves beyond multiple-choice testing to real-world application of knowledge. Let's examine the problem step-by-step to see how this can be done.

### Constructing Meaning

When students ask: "Why do I have to know this?" teachers cannot simply state: "Well, it is going to be on the test," or "Someday you will need to know this." That is not a motivating answer for most of today's students. Normally, the first step in a teacher's planning process is deciding the content objectives for the unit or lesson. Whether using teacher-created or state- and locally-mandated objectives, the teacher must figure out why it is important for students to learn the particular subject matter (academic content) in the lesson at hand. Thus, teachers need to think hard about the their course content and decide what is important for students to know and why it is important for them to know it.

Although this may seem obvious, it is not always easy. This is especially true given the nature of textbooks and state or local course curricula that tend to be "all inclusive" and chock-full of factual material that appears unlinked to any story line or pattern. Therefore, it is up to the teacher to help students construct meaning by understanding why they need to know the specific course content in the lesson or unit. Let us use an illustration from world history that many teachers have difficulty explaining. Why should a world history student need to learn about the provisions of the Peace of Westphalia for a test?

Remember, the Peace of Westphalia, 1648, was the treaty ending the Thirty Years' War in Europe. This corresponds to the *National Standards for World History*, Era 6, Standard 2B: Analyzing causes of religious wars in sixteenth and seventeenth century Europe and their effects on the establishment of religious pluralism (p. 176). The topic of the Thirty Years' War and the treaty are found in standard world history textbooks in the chapter relating to the rise of monarchies in Europe during the Renaissance and Reformation. The terms of this treaty in the German states, where most of the fighting took place, required people to adopt the religion of the Prince who ruled their State. The people were expected to convert if the ruler of the State changed his or her religion either through marriage, war, or conversion. Why would students want to learn this?

Maybe the point of the lesson should be less about memorizing facts relating to the Peace of Westphalia than about the issue of a treaty where an individual's religion is decided by the religion of the Prince in the State in which he or she resides. Once the teacher focuses on the broader issue, the lesson/unit objectives—in this example the required curriculum standard about the provisions of the Peace of Westphalia—can be embedded in a problem or a question that relates to the importance of the content rather than particular facts.

Simply, once the teacher figures out the importance of the content, he or she designs a question or problem that will enable the students to figure out this importance independently. In the Peace of Westphalia example, the questions for students to explore become: What would you do if a treaty were signed with the provision that your religion will be decided by the government rather than by your personal preference? Has this ever happened? What were the results? Could it happen today? Could it happen here in the U.S.? Students who are constructing meaning by answering these questions should be more motivated to learn the material because they are answering questions that they deem important or worth answering rather than simply memorizing facts about a treaty and a war they have little or no interest in.

## Using Disciplined Inquiry to Construct Meaning — activities, strategies

The teacher needs to assess what the skills or social science methodologies are that are necessary for students to solve the problem or answer the question(s) posed. For example, these could be:
- Reading a chart or a diagram;
- Explaining the chronology of the issue;
- Interpreting a map; or
- Using the scientific method for problem solving.

Because competent social studies/history teaching requires that every lesson includes a content component and a skills component, the perennial question of whether social studies teachers should be teaching content or process is solved. Do both. The students are engaged with the material by using the tools of inquiry and problem solving. They are operating as social scientists or historians while they master the course material required by either the national/state standards or the school district.

## Value or Meaning Beyond Success in School

It is important that the problem or question under study in the classroom be related to the real world as opposed to simply the realm of the scholar. Again, this relates to the first point about "meaning." When the teacher decides the "why" of the material, as in "why are we studying this?" that answer must be framed within the context of the real world. Then, with the teacher serving as a guide, the question or problem designed by the teacher is presented to the students to explore and to answer. In the previous example, the issue of how someone chooses their religion clearly has value and application beyond school.

## Producing Knowledge

In a well-designed, authentic task the student needs to acquire and utilize the desired academic content in order to create the product or find the answer to the problem posed. That means the student, not the teacher, is finding the meaning by locating the knowledge necessary in the context of the solution for the problem or the product created. The teacher designs a rubric or performance (product) evaluation sheet as part of the original assignment. In that way, the students are aware of what they are required to demonstrate to prove that they have learned the content at the same time that the question is posed.

In the example we have been using, the student might need to create a chart demonstrating the positives and negatives of the role of the government in religion. This chart might be started early in the world history course with the theocracy of ancient Egypt. Students could follow the issue throughout the year, adding to the chart at appropriate times during the course. For an end-of-course review, they might then be expected to use that chart to write an essay on the role of the state in religion.

Or, students could approach the world history course topically (thematically), and one of the topics or themes might be the role of the government in relation to religion. Then, the essay or a debate could become the culminating activity of the unit. The expectations or requirements of the learning outcome are presented at the start of the lesson when the problem/question is posed regardless of the performance or product the teacher selects. This will eliminate student questions about a fact's importance or if it will be on a test or not.

Figure 1.2 demonstrates how proper planning can achieve authentic instruction:

## Figure 1.2. The Planning Process

| | |
|---|---|
| Begin | with the objective(s) or standard to be learned. |
| Ask | Why is this objective important for my students to know? How does it connect to the real world concerns of students? What is the underlying issue this objective relates to? What essential question does this knowledge address? |
| Create | a problem statement or pose a question to address the importance of the factual knowledge or the essential question the objective addresses. |
| Select | the most appropriate way for students to demonstrate that they have learned the answer to the question or solved the problem. For example: an essay, a debate, a simulation, role-playing, research paper, poster, map, charts and graphs, etc. |
| Select | instructional strategy(ies) that helps the students to solve the problem or answer the questions posed. For example; cooperative learning groups, individual research, inquiry approach based on the steps of problem solving, etc. |
| Design | a rubric for evaluating student answers to the problem or questions posed. Incorporate the skills and the academic content needed to answer the question or solve the problem into the rubric design using the criteria for authentic assessment. |

## Criteria for Authentic Assessment

Newmann and Wehlage suggest that to design an assessment tool that meets the three criteria for authentic instruction, a teacher needs to examine five standards for authentic assessment. These five standards are used in evaluating any lesson, unit, or course by locating student performance along a continuum for each standard, thereby creating an assessment rubric. The idea of the continuum is to illustrate for students what excellent, very good, satisfactory, poor and unacceptable work looks like. In traditional terms, this continuum would provide benchmarks or examples of traditional grade categories with excellent representing "A," very good representing "B," and so on down the continuum. Thus, from the beginning of the assignment, students know exactly what they are supposed to learn, how they are to demonstrate that learning, and what acceptable work looks like. The standards teachers need to account for are:

- Higher-order thinking
- Depth of knowledge
- Connectedness to the world beyond the classroom
- Substantive conversation
- Social support for student achievement

What do each of these criteria represent?

## Higher-Order Thinking

Higher-order thinking means that students demonstrate their ability to understand content beyond simple memorization and repetition of facts. If we were to go back to the standard, Bloom's taxonomy (see Figure 1.3), we would find higher-order thinking at the top half of the pyramid.

### Figure 1.3. Bloom's Cognitive Taxonomy

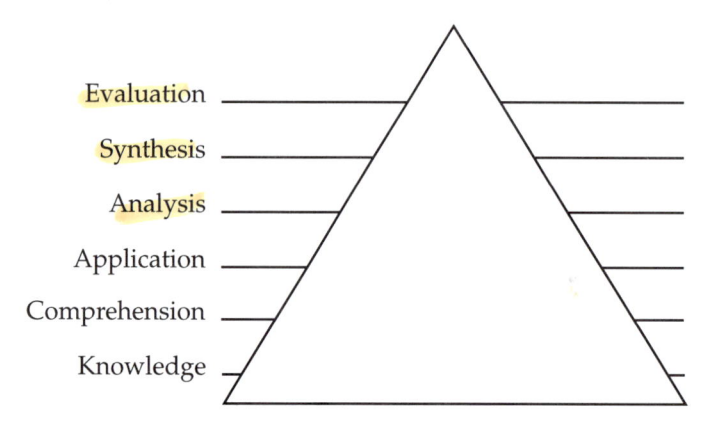

Evaluation
Synthesis
Analysis
Application
Comprehension
Knowledge

The inquiry approach, that is, asking questions or posing problems for authentic instruction, automatically brings students to the top of the pyramid. This relates to the criteria of authentic learning for creating meaning. Unless students have learned to analyze, synthesize, and evaluate course material, they are not creating meaning or producing knowledge.

## Depth of Knowledge

Criterion one, higher-order or critical thinking, is achieved partly by criterion two, depth of knowledge. Proof of critical thinking or problem solving comes from studying a problem in depth and displaying an understanding of a chain of evidence in order to explain the reasons for a problem or question posed by the teacher. The chain of evidence is created as students learn and apply historic events, geographic data, and study famous people or important concepts to answer questions or solve problems posed by the teacher.

In terms of the Thirty Years' War example, students would need to research the causes of the war including the Reformation, the rise of secular political power in Europe, and the results of the war, including the implementation of the treaty and it's effect on the people living in the area at the time. This encompasses geographic, social, and economic understandings of Germany in the time period, with its Catholic population as rural and inhabiting the southern part of the country, and its Protestant population being northern, more urbanized, more educated, and embracing the new economic system of capitalism.

This is considerably more depth than the traditional textbook and worksheet question require, even though this information is alluded to by many textbooks and is usually explained in filmstrips/videotapes covering the effects of the Protestant Reformation. It might even be more information than the typical world history teacher has at his or her fingertips. That is why the students are solving the problems and the teachers are simply guiding them to find sources for answers to the questions asked. Teachers should not be expected to have all the answers. But, teachers should be expected to help students figure out how and where to find the answers.

At this point, teachers might be concerned about the time it will take students to access the information and complete the product or performance required. This is especially true for a more obscure topic like the Thirty Years' War. Inquiry-based learning is always more time consuming than traditional lecture and worksheet-driven instruction. However, the time problem can be mitigated by using cooperative learning and by thematic or topical approaches to the curriculum. In addition, the fact that students are more interested should lead to more productivity, greater learning, and better retention of material, thereby raising grades in spite of a slower pace. To some extent, the teacher may need to make a decision that "less is more" and choose to omit some topics that seem to be less important to the curriculum than others.

## Connectedness to the Real World

The connectedness element focuses students and teachers on the real world application of the content being learned. Remember that earlier we established that the teacher would frame the problems or questions posed to students in the context of real-world concerns. In terms of our Peace of Westphalia example, these questions included: What would you do if a treaty were signed with the provision that your religion will be decided by the government rather than by your personal preference? Has this ever happened? What were the results? Could it happen today? Could it happen here in the U.S.? These questions are raised because our assessment criteria must include a place for students to demonstrate that they see and understand the connection with the real world. If we think about our religion and government example, at some point, in addition to knowing about the Thirty Year's War and the Peace of

Westphalia, the students might need to become familiar with the First Amendment to the U.S. Constitution and the rights they are guaranteed in this nation, as well as being able to cite examples of other nations that do not offer this insurance.

## Substantive Conversation

Substantive conversation is defined as the opportunity to engage in discussion with classmates and teachers to explore and display understanding of the topic under study. When students are focused on active learning and teachers are facilitating students engaged in inquiry and problem solving, this criterion becomes an easy element to integrate into the assessment rubric. The focus in this standard is with depth of knowledge demonstrated by students using the language of historians/social scientists as problems are studied.

Referring back to Bloom's taxonomy (Figure 1.3), the teacher asks probing questions that bring students to the higher-order thinking skills. Probing questions are questions that go beyond factual recall and push students to understand the how and why of history. Teachers will need to practice asking this type of question and develop skills with framing questions over time. Students will need to engage in discussion with peers as well as with the teacher in order to supply answers to the questions being asked. This process yields "substantive conversation," as opposed to the more superficial recitation in traditional lecture-based, drill-and-practice instructional methodologies. The use of cooperative learning strategies provides one mechanism for creating opportunities for substantive conversation.

## Social Support

Social support for student achievement refers to the fact that peers and teachers are involved with helping the student in her or his search for answers and production or performance of the solution to any problem posed. Remember, placing the teacher in the role of the facilitator, instead of the "giver of truth," ensures that conversation will occur. This is a change from traditional classroom procedures.

At first, students may be uncomfortable with this new approach to learning because it will require more effort from them than the passive listening, recitation, or worksheets they are accustomed to in their history classes. Thus, to make this work, teachers and peers in the class need to positively reinforce each other as they take the risk of entering into the realm of inquiry. Students may be hesitant to raise questions or to attempt answers to seemingly difficult questions. As authentic instruction moves students from simply knowing "what" or "that"—the lowest levels on Bloom's triangle—to thinking about and knowing "why" and "how," students may be unsure of how to proceed. Providing social support becomes a criterion for assessment as students are expected to assist one another as they display their products or present their performances at the end of a unit of study.

## Other Views of Authentic Instruction and Assessment

Although we have been focusing on Newmann's work, there are other researchers who are also concerned with authentic teaching and learning. Gordon's (1998) criteria for authentic learning requires students to:

- Actively solve problems
- Work together
- Be placed in a learning situation that simultaneously involves one's knowledge, skills, and attitudes
- Be driven by "essential knowledge" that is meaningful to students (concerned with the big questions of humanity)
- Participate in activities that are connected
- Publicly exhibit their learning using real-life standards of quality

Authentic assessment is an extension of this concept. Wiggins (1990) states that authentic assessment requires students to be effective performers, with acquired knowledge mirroring the same concerns and challenges found in top-notch instruction:

- Research
- Writing
- Revision
- Discussion and analyis
- Collaboration

Although there are small differences in the stated criteria, the approaches are very similar. Thus, both authentic instruction and authentic assessment strategies seek to have students go beyond mere absorption and regurgitation of academic knowledge to utilization and production of that knowledge to create new and meaningful products.

## An Interdisciplinary Approach

The teaching of history/social studies requires an interdisciplinary approach to subject matter if the student is to reach understanding or find meaning and connection to the real world. As a history teacher, I used to show my students a conceptual framework, or approach to the study of history, that we used throughout the year to help them increase their understanding of the course. This framework consisted of examining each unit topic under study from the following aspects: political, economic, religious, social, intellectual and aesthetic (the arts). We used an acronym, PERSIA, to help remember these words. Using these concepts as an organizer for the course made it easier for students to understand and make meaning out of the facts and events of history. They could discover patterns and understand how seemingly disparate events really made sense when examined from multiple perspectives.

Consider all the data that students needed to gather to understand the Thirty Years' War questions discussed earlier in this chapter. How would the PERSIA framework have enabled students to approach the task and gather the information efficiently? A chart could be created with columns for entering political, economic, religious social, intellectual and geographic (in this case) information. The rows could include causes of the war, results of the treaty, etc. If more than one war or country were under study, the chart could be configured with those topics as rows. Students could fill in the information that is necessary and use the chart that they create to answer the original question/problem posed by the teacher.

These types of graphic organizers work well with authentic instruction and authentic assessment because they make it easy to design tasks for students that meet the criteria necessary for higher-order thinking. Several lesson plans in this book present additional organizers in the form of scoring rubrics to aid students in locating information effectively.

## Standards: National, State, and Local

Returning to the time question, you may be wondering how authentic instruction will be possible in this age of school reform and teacher/student accountability. If students have to pass "high-stakes" multiple-choice tests in order to receive course credit and to graduate, how will teachers have time to use authentic learning strategies? As previously stated, if students actually use the course material to solve meaningful problems, they will increase their retention. This will lead to higher scores on their standardized tests.

Nonetheless, it will be necessary to include some practice throughout the school term on successful test-taking skills and to occasionally use traditional tests during the course. The goal here is balance. Simple drill and practice, with traditional lecture and worksheet instructional strategies, will not improve test scores if students are unmotivated, uninterested, and inattentive. Authentic instruction places students at the center of their learning, and this should yield the test scores needed for graduation while simultaneously providing learning experiences that will be meaningful and useful after graduation.

## Technology

How does technology fit into this picture? It will be easier for teachers to design and provide authentic learning units and lessons by utilizing some of the new software and Internet-based learning programs that are increasingly more available. These technologies make it easier for students to become problem solvers and for teachers to become facilitators. Most of the lessons in this book include Web-based resources to point the way for teachers to merge authentic learning with computers. If the teacher does not have access to the Internet during class or enough computers for students to share, then the teacher needs to bring the Internet to the students by downloading and printing out information from the sites listed in the lesson plans. In this way, students can access valuable online information despite the lack of technology in their classrooms.

## Putting It All Together

Why bother to use authentic instruction and authentic assessment or performance-based instructional strategies for teaching history/social studies? Won't this be a lot of work for both the teacher and the students? Although this will initially entail more work for teachers, in the long run, adopting these methods will make the teacher's life easier, not harder. In working with both pre-service and in-service teachers, the common complaint is that the most difficult part of lesson/unit design is the step that requires the teacher to decide what essential question or issue is contained in the objective/standard to be taught. To address this difficulty, some curriculum guides now contain the essential questions. In fact, some curriculum guides now state not only the essential question for each objective, but also the essential knowledge that students need to answer the question. The task for the teacher becomes deciding whether or not the questions and knowledge listed are truly the important or essential issues that the objective incorporates. If not, the teacher must rethink the issues the objective raises.

In a well-designed lesson, students will become the active learners and teachers the facilitators or guides to that learning. As students become more involved in their learning and see the relevance of their studies to their lives, motivation should increase and discipline problems should decrease. This is not to say that all of the teacher's problems will be solved. Rather, it is saying that at a time when teaching is becoming an ever more difficult and stressful job, adopting performance-based learning strategies can help make the job more rewarding and assist teachers in becoming more professional in their teaching.

# 2
# Authentic Tasks and Rubrics

## The Limits of Traditional Assessment

The first issue to deal with is why traditional forms of assessment alone are an inadequate way of determining student knowledge. This is particularly true for the "standard" multiple-choice exams that are so popular in schools. It is possible to create or to find multiple-choice questions that bring students to higher levels of thinking as delineated by Bloom's taxonomy. But, most traditional test questions rely on the simple regurgitation of the factual content that was taught through teacher lecture, textbook readings and the concurrent worksheets or exercises provided with the chapters. This keeps students on the lower levels of Bloom's pyramid because the test questions only emphasize knowing "that" or "what." Thus, students are not stimulated to either apply the knowledge or utilize it to produce new knowledge, including making evaluations or inferences about the importance or meaning of the content under study. In other words, students may memorize factual material and pass tests, but the tests do not ensure that the students understand what they have memorized.

Thus, although nobody questions the importance of attaining a knowledge base, the downfall of traditional short-answer tests (multiple-choice, true or false, fill in the blank) is that they do not focus students on what Wiggins (1999, speech to VASCD) calls the "Essential Questions." Students who master the factual content might be successful on a knowledge-based TV game show such as "Jeopardy," but beyond that, the course material has little value or utility. Simply gearing one's teaching toward mastering factual content provides little incentive for students to master this content, even with the threat of high-stakes exit tests needed for graduation. Unfortunately, many students seem not to care about graduation, especially those we need to be most concerned with in terms of accountability. Additionally, assuming that the students do master the content, how does that knowledge further the underlying mission of the social studies to prepare students for active, democratic citizenship?

Even if a teacher were to include an essay question on the exam, unless that question were geared toward utilization of the factual knowledge needed to produce new knowledge or to attain the highest level of Bloom's pyramid, that test would still be considered a traditional assessment. Thus, it is not only the kind of question asked, but also the type of information required for the answer that moves assessment from the traditional to the authentic realm.

## The Benefits of Authentic, Performance-Based Assessment

Recall Newmann and Wehlage's (1993) criteria for authentic assessment (see Chapter 1):

- Constructing meaning and producing knowledge
- Using disciplined inquiry to construct meaning
- Aiming schoolwork toward production or performance that has value or meaning beyond success in school (high grades)

These three criteria ensure that in addition to mastering the knowledge base (factual course content), the students are also doing so for a purpose—the construction of meaning and for real-life value regardless of their future career choices. This relates to factors that the United States government has deemed important for students to know and be able to do upon graduation as explained by the SCANS report.

The SCANS (Secretary's Commission on Achieving Necessary Skills) report, *What Work Requires of Schools* (1991, 1992), was issued by the U.S. Secretary of Labor upon recommendations from a task force commissioned to determine what knowledge and abilities are necessary for success in the world of work. It is important that high school teachers include these skills and competencies in their instruction. This is especially true for students who are not planning on four-year college and/or graduate school. SCANS identifies the following basic skills as being necessary for success after school.

- **Basic Skills:**
  - Reads, writes, performs arithmetic and mathematical operations, listens and speaks well.
- **Thinking Skills:**
  - Thinks creatively, makes decisions, solves problems, visualizes, knows how to learn, and reasons well.
- **Personal Qualities:**
  - Displays responsibility, self-esteem, sociability, self-management, and integrity and honesty.

In addition, SCANS identifies five workplace competencies.

- **Resources:**
  - Identifies, organizes, plans, and allocates the resources (time, money, materials and facilities, and human resources).
- **Interpersonal:**

# Authentic Tasks and Rubrics

- Works with others as a member of a team, including contributing to the group, teaching others new skills, serving clients/customers, exercising leadership, negotiating, and working with diversity.
- Information:
  - Acquires and uses information, organizes and maintains information, interprets and communicates information, and uses computers to process information.
- Systems:
  - Understands complex interrelationships, including monitoring and repairing systems that are not working.
- Technology:
  - Works with a variety of technologies, including selecting, maintaining and troubleshooting equipment as needed.

Authentic instruction in both the learning and assessment phases allows teachers to assist their students in mastering these skills and competencies. Attention to SCANS skills has the advantage of helping teachers to more efficiently and effectively design lessons with real-world application. It is helpful for teachers to share the SCANS requirements with the students at the beginning of the school term and to remind them of the need to focus on the development of these skills and competencies throughout the year. Directing attention to these skills reinforces the need to understand and apply the content being learned in social studies class.

## Reaching Out to Others

Teachers might be wondering how they can accomplish all of this within the amount of teacher planning time allotted by most school districts. Whenever embarking on a new project, learning experience, or course assignment, extra time is always necessary. However, as with the time it took the teacher to master the traditional format, once the change to authentic learning is made, planning time decreases to a reasonable amount. One suggestion is to begin to integrate authentic instruction slowly, one unit at a time over a period of two to three years. This technique gives teachers reflective time to improve activities and assessments without overwhelming the teachers with new procedures.

Another suggestion is to envision some assignments as multidisciplinary or interdisciplinary, depending on the topic under study and on colleagues' interests. Then teachers could plan in concert with one or more colleagues, making the design and assessment of the unit a shared responsibility. A side benefit of this approach is that the teachers are modeling the collaborative approach called for in the SCANS discussion above. We next define the differences between these two approaches: multidisciplinary and interdisciplinary.

Using a multidisciplinary approach means that any given topic or idea can be studied in more than one subject area simultaneously, thus adding depth and breath of understanding of the topic or concept. Social studies teachers already implement some of this because the social studies department usually offers courses in geography, history, government (and/or civics), and economics. Within these course offerings, often the same topics are studied, but frequently the emphases are a little different. The PERSIA organizer discussed in Chapter 1 uses a multidisciplinary approach to history/social studies learning.

On a broader scale, a concept like "space" could be explored in science class as "outer space;" in world history class as Hitler's concept of *lebensraum* ("living room") or in U.S. history as the frontier; in English class as individual space (Virginia Woolf's *A Room of One's Own*); in math class as area, etc. Using this approach, the teachers involved could assign one culminating project in which a student or group of students demonstrate their understandings of the concept of "space." The teachers would agree on the components necessary for an authentic project's successful completion and share in the evaluation responsibilities.

This is most successful when the teachers share the same group of students. However, even if the exact same students are not in each class, the integration of the concept into several subjects will become clear as students who have the classes that overlap discuss their ideas with classmates not assigned to all of the same teachers. This approach signifies that the various subject teachers will address the concept but not necessarily at the same time or in the same manner.

The interdisciplinary approach requires more integration of the concept under study and closer cooperation among the teachers involved. For instance, social studies teachers usually need to teach map skills. A basic concept of map work is that of latitude and longitude. To understand this concept, it is necessary for students to become aware of the fact that these imaginary lines form a grid, similar to a graph in mathematics class. Any specific location on a map—the intersection of the latitude and the longitude—is plotted by locating its relationship on the "x" and "y" axes.

What would happen if the math teacher teamed up with the geography and history teachers and taught graphing using maps? The teachers would then design and assign a single project for which students would receive a grade in each of the classes. This becomes authentic because students need to use maps throughout their lives as they travel outside of their home to any new place (either locally, nationally, or internationally). Here again, the teachers collaborate in designing and evaluating the projects so the work involved for one individual teacher decreases while student learning, understanding and making connections increases.

Remember, the first time the assignment is planned and implemented, it will require extra time, but after the initial design and revision, the workload should decrease. Technology, such as e-mail with word-processed attachments, serves to make this collaboration more efficient because teachers can work asynchronously during their assigned planning periods, which cuts down the need for multiple face-to-face meetings.

## Understanding Curriculum Alignment

In order to successfully collaborate, or to design an individual authentic assignment, teachers need to understand curriculum alignment. As previously stated in Chapter 1, in its simplest form, curriculum alignment can be described as deciding what you want to teach (your objectives or outcomes), teaching to those objectives or outcomes, then testing achievement of those objectives or outcomes. Again, how many times has a student asked: "Is this going to be on the test?" Curriculum alignment requires the teacher to think about the assessment before beginning the teaching.

Teachers might be thinking, "isn't this simply teaching to the test?" The answer is "no" for two reasons:

1. Knowing that your desired objectives or outcomes are incorporated into your assessment before you design and present your lessons ensures that the daily lessons do achieve the desired goals; and

2. If you are designing authentic, performance-based assessments, there is no way to "teach to the test" because each student's product will be unique.

What the teacher is doing is communicating about what he or she wishes students to achieve, and then creating assignments that will guide them toward success. In addition, it is not necessarily wrong to be teaching "to the test" if the test is meaningful and important. Because authentic assessments need to be meaningful and important by definition, this should not be a problem.

The planning becomes easier to accomplish if the teacher steps back from the "What do I do on Monday?" frame of mind and takes a longer view. Ask, "When my students leave my class at the end of the school year, what do I want them to know and be able to do?" It is at this point that a teacher might consult the SCANS Report and/or the NCSS (National Council for the Social Studies) Standards, as well as their state or local curriculum guides, to think about the larger purposes behind the study of any particular academic area of social studies. Generally, these larger aims, usually called "goals" can be found in the mission statement or introductory materials in the front of these curriculum guides.

Consulting these documents provides a sort of check or reinforcement for the teacher. Performing this check helps the teacher to be sure that in deciding what students should know and be able to do, she or he hasn't left out something important. In the end, the teacher makes the decision on what to teach (Thornton, 1989) because it is the teacher who is alone in the room with the students. All the standards documents, curriculum guides, high-stakes tests, etc. cannot, in the end, control the final say of what actually gets taught in the individual classroom; the teacher is the curricular-instructional gatekeeper.

Another method of checking is to focus on Wiggins' Essential Questions (1999). It is important to remember that many curriculum guides list "big" or essential questions that are neither big nor essential. When reading a curriculum guide, the teacher needs to ask: "Is this truly an essential or important idea?" If the answer is yes, then that goal is worthy of adoption.

Once the course goals are selected, it becomes easier for teachers to do two things: (a) design goals and objectives (outcomes) for individual units and lessons; and (b) to check to see that these sub-goals and objectives are aligned with the course goals. Even where there is a traditional state exam at the end of the course, the state curriculum guide for that course has stated goals and objectives. If the teacher keeps those goals in mind, then authentic learning methodologies can be implemented while still preparing students to pass standardized tests. Thus, the course is more relevant and useful to students while simultaneously ensuring that they master the factual content needed to pass the state exit test.

## Designing Authentic Performance Tasks and Assessments

How do teachers go about actually designing authentic learning lessons and tasks? Traditionally, teachers separate daily learning tasks and activities from formal assessments. Be aware that with careful initial planning, there will not necessarily be separate tasks and assessments in authentic learning situations. The components (tasks) may all be part of the final project. In other words, as teachers design the assessment project, the tasks that are the component parts will fall into place. Students will be aware from day one what they need to accomplish, and at what level of mastery it needs to be accomplished, to complete the work satisfactorily.

As in traditional lesson planning, teachers begin with unit goals and objectives thinking: i.e., "What do I want students to know and be able to do when they complete this unit of study?" Remember that teachers need to include cognitive (factual content), affective (feeling, attitude, or disposition), and social studies skills goals for students. Because traditional social studies lessons require these same categories of objectives/outcomes, nothing has really changed yet. The change comes in trying to be sure that the overarching goals that the students are mastering deal with essential questions linked to the real world. Let us look at a simple example that might bridge the gap from traditional to authentic assessment as a place to start.

Traditionally, students in world history (and often government) classes study the Greek city-state of Athens as a democracy. Given that we live in a representative democracy, an authentic task would have students evaluate Athenian democracy by comparing it to democracies in other places and ages, including our own. This task deals with the essential question "What do we mean by the words 'democratic form of government?'" In order to successfully answer this question, students would have to be able to formulate a list of criteria—the attributes of democracy—with which to test any given government.

Instead of the teacher lecturing to the students or having them read about ancient Athens in the textbook and then answering a worksheet, the students are charged with the following task (works most effectively in cooperative learning groups): Establish a list of at least five characteristics by which we can determine whether or not any given government is a democracy. For world history, apply that list to the following governments: ancient Athens, ancient Sparta, the Roman Republic, the Roman Empire, and

# Authentic Tasks and Rubrics

the United States. For a government class, the teacher can select five contemporary governments for students to research. For a U.S. history class, the teacher could focus on different time periods, such as the eras of Jefferson, Jackson, Lincoln, Wilson, F.D. Roosevelt, L. Johnson, etc.

The students could use a jigsaw cooperative learning strategy (students belong to both expert groups and to home groups) to complete the task. The project might integrate technology by requiring students to prepare a multimedia presentation (PowerPoint or Hyperstudio) for the class that would demonstrate their findings. There could also be a culminating class discussion or debate on the question: "How democratic is the United States government today?" Or, in light of recent historic events, "How many of our democratic rights can we sacrifice in time of war and still be labeled a 'democracy'?"

The first step would be for each home group to establish the criteria for assessing the level of democracy of a government. Then, the teacher could have the class reach a consensus on that list or let each group pursue its own list. Letting each group pursue its own list would enable students to discover whether some criteria would be more valid than others in assessing democracy. This provides students with almost complete control over the inquiry process. If the teacher is not comfortable giving students that much control, the criteria list could be provided or the class consensus method could be implemented.

The students could then move to expert groups. Using the world history example, there would be an expert group for Athens, Sparta, the Roman Republic, the Roman Empire, and the U.S. Each group would research the criteria for democracy in relation to the government assigned to them. Students undertake their research by using library and computer resources as well as their textbooks and any resources the teacher may have compiled in the classroom. Once the expert groups complete the research and verify its accuracy, the expert groups break up and students return to their home group. Each home group has an "expert" responsible for teaching the other students in their home group the most important facts about the specific government studied.

Because cooperative learning requires both individual accountability and group interdependence, the final tasks could include individual essays as well as the group presentation. These essays would be based on specific criteria for writing essays, and would require students to evaluate the governments studied by making some comparisons as well as tracing changes in our ideas of democracy over time. Another way to achieve individual accountability would be through the use of the group multimedia presentation mentioned earlier. The presentation can complete the unit, with each group member preparing the "slide" that covers his or her assigned government.

How does this task meet the criteria for authentic learning?

- First, by constructing meaning and producing knowledge. Each group will reach its own list of the attributes of democracy and apply that list to various governments of the teacher's choosing. For the world history and the U.S. history examples, the governments above were selected for their chronological proximity in the traditional history course that would align easily with most state/local curricula, but the teacher is free to select other governments/time periods. As the students are working in groups, researching the selected governments, and applying the criteria, they are producing the knowledge and constructing the meaning.

- Second, by using disciplined inquiry to construct meaning. The students are using social science, critical thinking/problem solving strategies when they draw up a list of attributes of the concept "democracy" and then seek to apply the factual content to answer the original question: "What do we mean by the words 'democratic government'?"
- Third, by aiming schoolwork toward production or performance that has value or meaning beyond success in school (high grades), students are learning several things in this exercise that meet this criterion. They are:
  - Learning to work in groups.
  - Working on communication skills, both oral and written.
  - Learning or practicing technology skills.
  - Working on research and reading comprehension skills as they seek the factual knowledge to support the criteria of democracy they selected.
  - Learning the factual content that makes up the component parts of democracy, an important knowledge base for our future citizens.

Notice that although the teacher may have had more work in the initial stages of the planning, when it comes to the daily work of teaching, the teacher has become a facilitator circulating and assisting the groups in locating information and staying on task. The students are now actively involved in their own learning: creating meaning, and solving problems that are relevant to their lives.

Initially, this can be difficult for students because it changes their expectations of what will happen in class. Over time, as students become familiar with active learning, discipline problems should decrease and motivation should increase because the class is no longer a passive recipient of knowledge but the creator of the knowledge. After all, active, involved students have less time to create problems. Good teachers have known this for as long as there have been teachers.

There is one concern a teacher may have at this point. Despite the individual essay, how can a teacher be sure that all the students have learned all the factual information when each student was a member of only one expert group? As the transition is made to authentic learning, to feel secure and understand that each student is responsible for learning the material that his/her classmates are presenting, teachers should still give some quizzes, tests, etc., on the factual content to reinforce that point. In fact, in states where traditional multiple-choice testing is the norm, teachers would be remiss if they did not provide students with some opportunity to practice traditional question formats. After all, if they don't pass the tests, they won't graduate. That is also a real-world connection!

Further, most teachers do not make a full switch from traditional to authentic classroom overnight. As suggested earlier, teachers might consider phasing in authentic learning lessons and units over time, possibly even years, until they feel comfortable with these instructional strategies.

# Designing Evaluation Rubrics

A range of instruments can be designed to fit the criteria of an evaluation rubric. Newmann and Associates (1996, p. 29) present a list of standards necessary for authentic assessment tasks. This list is broken into three sections with two standards in each section as follows:

- Construction of Knowledge
  - *Organization of information.* This requires students to present their solutions to the assigned task in complex ways that reach the highest level of critical thinking.
  - *Consideration of alternatives.* Students must account for multiple strategies and perspectives in explaining the information or problem solution.
- Disciplined Inquiry
  - *Disciplinary content.*
  - *Disciplinary process.* Students must use the tools and methods of social science to uncover the historic factual content learned and presented.
  - *Elaborated written communication* (oral communication could be substituted). Students must back up opinions with evidence in extended written form as well as verbally.
- Value beyond School
  - *Problem connected to the world beyond the classroom.*
  - *Audience beyond the school.* In addition to a concern with real world problems, the optimal authentic assessment assignment would include an outside audience invited to attend and judge the presentation portion of the project.

Although this may be the optimum that teachers strive to reach, it is unrealistic to think that all assignments will be designed to insure that these criteria are met. The best way to approach authentic assessment is to begin slowly and work towards the ideal performance criteria listed above. Especially in states with standardized curriculum and high-stakes testing, it might be difficult for the teacher to find the class time needed to complete an assignment that meets all the above criteria.

Evaluation rubrics can vary from scoring instruments that award traditional point values based on assignment criteria to holistic statements accompanied by examples (benchmarks) illustrating each category of performance. Figure 2.1 takes the format of a scoring rubric as it breaks down the assignment requirements and awards points for completion of each category. The number of points per category relates to the importance of the requirement to the successful completion of the assignment. In addition, the "points possible" column enables the teacher to differentiate levels of performance in the "points earned" column. The assignment can total to as many points as the teacher prefers. The simplest format is to have the point total equal 100, but this is not the teacher's only option. Teachers may use any number of points they choose. Notice that there are evaluation categories for daily tasks and behaviors needed to complete the assignment in addition to the final presentation.

## Figure 2.1. Democratic Governments Project Grading Rubric

|  | Tasks | Points Possible | Points Earned |
|---|---|---|---|
| *Group work* |  |  |  |
| Home Group | Criteria for democracy |  |  |
|  | Multimedia presentation |  |  |
|  | * Intro with criteria |  |  |
|  | * Athens |  |  |
|  | * Sparta |  |  |
|  | * Roman Republic |  |  |
|  | * Roman Empire |  |  |
|  | * United States |  |  |
|  | * Conclusion |  |  |
|  | * Design (color, font, spelling/ grammar) |  |  |
| *Expert Group* |  |  |  |
| Role | Research |  |  |
|  | Communication |  |  |
|  | * Oral |  |  |
|  | * Written |  |  |
| Individual Essay |  |  |  |
|  | Thesis statement |  |  |
|  | Defines terms |  |  |
|  | 3 examples |  |  |
|  | 2 facts for each example |  |  |
|  | Conclusion |  |  |
|  | Grammar, spelling, style |  |  |
| Class Discussion |  |  |  |
|  | Participation |  |  |
|  | * Respect for other speakers |  |  |
|  | * Contribution to discussion |  |  |
|  | Total |  |  |

*Comments: (can include teacher assessment of group and individual work, attendance, participation; evaluations from group members about the students, etc.)*

# Authentic Tasks and Rubrics 23

As teachers and students become comfortable with authentic instruction, grading rubrics can become more holistic. For example, rather than the point scoring format listed for the individual essay, a teacher might provide samples of essays that illustrate what an "A," "B," "C," etc., look like. Students would read the samples and notice that an "A" essay:

- Has a thesis statement;
- Defines terms, lists examples and evidence to back up opinions or to prove points;
- Makes few factual errors;
- Has a conclusion; and
- Uses appropriate grammar, spelling, and style.

Rather than awarding points for each of the above criteria, the total essay is read and a grade assigned based on the presence or the absence of those features. Teachers can review the benchmark essays with students to insure that the specific criteria have been understood.

The sample lesson plans in this book use a variety of scoring instruments to assist teachers in developing rubrics that they are comfortable with. In general, if the teacher reviews the tasks that make up the components of the assignment and accounts for these tasks in the rubric, then the rubric will successfully evaluate the assignment. This includes accounting for the social studies content, the social studies skills being learned or practiced, and the attitudes of dispositions being addressed by the assignment.

## Communicating with Students and Parents about Grades

Traditionally teachers give tests, grade homework or notebooks (or both), and sometimes add grades for class participation, attendance, etc. Although the assignment described above is fairly traditional, we can nevertheless begin to alter our grading patterns to move toward the place where the assignments and the grades may become much less traditional. Remember that providing students with the grading rubric at the outset places both students and their parents in a "comfort zone" because everyone knows what is required to be successful in class. It would be helpful for the teacher to explain the purposes and criteria for authentic learning to parents, either in a letter or on "Open House Night" when parents come to meet their child's teachers. This way, parents are clear about what the teacher requires without having to rely on their child to explain these changes in the system.

The scoring rubric for the democratic government example (Figure 2.1) is a simple chart, with the components of the project listed with some weighted value attached to each component. The teacher outlines the different assignments and tasks each student will have to complete and determines how many points could be awarded for each task. The number of points the student actually receives will be entered in the last column and totaled for a project grade. As previously mentioned, this is only one type of possible rubric, but it was selected as an example that attempts to bridge the gap from traditional assessments by awarding points on a traditional grading scale. The points can be converted to letter grades quite easily.

Notice that the subcomponents for task completion have been included. For instance, if the teacher expects a traditional five-paragraph individual essay, regardless of the specific question asked, the essay will require a thesis statement, definition of terms, etc. Thus, students know from the outset what they must do to achieve the grade they desire.

For the multimedia presentation, by including a slide for each government, each group member should create that slide from the knowledge they gained in the expert group; thus the necessary group interdependence is assured. Again, it should be noted that this is not the only format the rubric might take; it is only one example. The "points possible" column has not been completed because that is left to the teacher's discretion.

Frequently, when students do group work, it can be helpful to provide students with separate evaluation sheets that they are required to complete with information assessing:

- Their role as a group member (expert and home group)
- Their contribution to the project
- Their feelings about the group in general (did it work well, was anyone not doing his/her job, etc.)

It is advisable to include a space on the project or assignment rubric or in the comments section to adjust the total grade based on the responses to this personal/group evaluation. That way, if all the group members report that one student did not contribute his or her fair share, the teacher has a mechanism to respond to that complaint. Additionally, the teacher can make notes on student behavior during their daily work on the project. Those notes can either transfer to the comments section or find a place in the rubric by adding a category with points awarded or detracted for daily work.

In any case, in addition to the point scale, the teacher should take the time to add written comments about the student's performance to the bottom of the rubric sheet. This makes it clear to both students and their parents that the points were not awarded arbitrarily but were based on requirements and the teacher's evaluation of the student's performance on the project components. If a more holistic rubric is used, copies of the samples or benchmarks should be available for parents as well as students to review. Clear communication among all parties is an important element of successful authentic instruction.

## Conclusion

As we close out this chapter, it should be noted that there is a difference between alternative assessment and authentic assessment. The goal of this book is not simply to substitute performance tasks and rubrics for multiple-choice or traditional forms of assessment. Alternative simply means asking students to do something a different way—there is no attempt to link the task to real-world concerns. As teachers consider moving toward authentic performance-based tasks and their accompanying rubrics, they need to keep in mind the three criteria defined in terms of what social studies teachers in general, and the classroom teacher in specific, want students to know and be able to do.

There are as many forms of rubrics as there is the imagination to design them. In the lesson examples that follow in Chapter 4, the rubric designs vary to provide examples of the range of options. The teacher needs to experiment, tinker with the format, and make it fit his or her specific needs. Remember, as the teacher moves from point-graded rubrics to those that contain the tasks assigned in one column with "benchmarks" or examples of expected performance in each grade category (this is what an "A" looks like, a "B," etc.), the most important consideration is how to design a rubric that takes into account the goals of the unit or lesson. Eventually, the teacher can move from letter grades to grading categories such as "excellent," "developing," "needs improvement," or "exceptional, admirable, acceptable, amateur" (http://www.phschool.com/professional_development/assessment/rub_coop_process.html).

The suggestion is to start with rubrics based on the samples in the book, and over time, adjust them until you feel confident enough to design your own. Whether designing your own rubrics, or locating already developed rubrics in resources such as social studies guides or on the Internet, it is important to keep some general criteria for evaluating rubrics in mind. According to *Evaluating Rubrics* published by the Chicago Public Schools, http://intranet.cps.k12.il.us/Assessments/Ideas_and_Rubrics/Intro_Scoring/Eval_Rubrics/eval_rubrics.html), as you select or design rubrics, be mindful of the following factors:

- Does the rubric relate to the learning objectives being measured?
- Does the rubric cover the important dimensions of student performance?
- Are the categories or benchmarks well defined?
- Is there a clear basis for assigning scores at each scale point (validity)?
- Can the rubric be applied consistently by different scorers (reliability)?
- Can the rubric be understood by students and parents?
- Is the rubric appropriate for the developmental level of the students?
- Can the rubric be applied to a variety of tasks and then adapted for a specific assignment (consistency of expectations)?
- Is the rubric fair and free from bias?
- Is the rubric useful, feasible, manageable and practical? Does it make sense to use it in the classroom?

With these factors in mind, good luck in working with the lessons presented in the following chapters.

# 3

# Integrating Performance Tasks and Rubrics: FAQ's

This chapter will take the form of frequently asked questions (FAQ's). Hopefully, using this format will enable concise answers to issues or points of concern that teachers may be having as they consider making the switch from traditional to authentic learning strategies.

## Will I Be Changing My Whole Course?

It is my guess that many teachers are already assigning interesting projects or teaching some lessons that could fit with the authentic learning criteria. I suggest building on those lessons by beginning to experiment with several of the lessons in this book that fit their curricula. I have tried to select lessons that use technology for teachers who need lessons that integrate technology standards. Also, the lessons in this book are centered on curriculum topics for which it tends to be difficult to find resources or to provide ideas for those areas where teachers might have knowledge gaps.

Beginning to use authentic instruction and authentic assessment with just one unit will raise a teacher's comfort level. Just remember that there are few concerns to be aware of:

- Daring to break out of the traditional mold and trying something new. This can be risky, especially if a teacher's colleagues are not trying this also. Sometimes the culture of the school makes it difficult to initiate new ideas.
- Becoming accustomed (as the teacher) to having the student, rather than the teacher, doing the bulk of the daily work. It takes time to switch from asking and answering the questions to only asking them and guiding students toward finding the answers themselves.
- Getting the students accustomed to having them, rather than the teacher, doing the bulk of the daily work. It is easier to have the

teacher supply the answer than for the student to dig for it. Students may rebel at first.

- ♦ Planning carefully to ensure the success of the lesson, unit or project. The old cliché "the devil is in the details" is apropos here. The success of authentic learning projects is rooted in careful planning.

Remember, the traditional social studies program is generally hated by students and labeled boring and meaningless. Do you really want to spend your teaching career being boring and meaningless? Do you want your students to find boring and meaningless the subject you loved enough to make a career of? So, dare to break the mold. Understand that it is always scary to be the first (or the only) member of the faculty or the department to try something new. There are voices that will tell you that the traditional way is best because it has always been done that way, etc. Why should you be bothered with this?

Why did you become a social studies teacher? Why do you think social studies is important? How can you communicate that in a way that students will understand? Well, you can't tell them! Students must become actively involved in creating meaning, and you must facilitate that. This is why you should dare to experiment. Besides, it might re-invigorate your love of the subject matter and make your days on the job more exciting, interesting, and, in the long run, less stressful.

## Will This Be Too Much Work Given All My Other Teacher Duties?

Let's combine the workload issues. First, for the teacher there is more work "up front" in unit and lesson design. But there is less work, and much less repetitive work, on a daily basis. For most teachers, the opposite is the general pattern. Instead of giving a lecture with recitation, which can be very tiring, the teacher gets to circulate and work with students on an individual and small group basis.

Do you really enjoy saying the same things three to five times each day? Asking the same questions, getting the same "I don't know" responses? Switching some of the teaching to authentic learning and assessment strategies will place the daily responsibility on the students. They have the responsibility to learn the material, to complete the tasks and the project components. They need to formulate the questions to find answers to the original assignment or question the teacher posed.

Teachers have the opportunity to move around from group to group, facilitating students' work. On a daily basis, this is much less stressful on the teacher and frequently more interesting as the teacher gets to interact with and know the students better.

## Will the Students Want to Work This Hard?

For the students, this will be a very big change. They will often resist this new approach at first because they are patterned to sit back and let you do all the work. They may even tell the teacher that he or she is "not teaching." Or, that you are "not getting paid to point them towards finding answers; you should know the answers and tell them." The idea of actually engaging in the work and doing the learning is a difficult concept, especially for students who have been successful in the traditional classroom. They have mastered the game and you are changing the rules!

So, be prepared in the beginning to nudge students along. Start with an assignment from the included lessons that you find particularly relevant or exciting. The students should have time allotted for debriefing, a discussion following the project, where they speak about their feelings about authentic versus traditional learning. Be prepared to explain why you have embarked on this new path and what you hope students will gain.

A plus is that the nontraditional, experiential and/or noncompetitive learners will generally prefer authentic instruction because working in groups is more social. Well-designed groups can be both fun and productive. The modern world of work that students will soon enter is usually not a passive place, but one where the successful worker takes some initiative for getting the job done, etc.

In other words, in the beginning, teachers may have to sell the program to the students. As they get used to it, even with the extra work that falls on them, students should find themselves excited and interested about coming to class. Note: this doesn't happen overnight! Give yourself and the students time to adjust.

## We Have Standardized State Exams. How Can I Find Time for These Projects?

Teachers need to stop thinking about performance-based lessons and units as add-ons when the teaching-for-the test "work is done." This sort of thinking sounds like "after the exam is over, we can do a unit that will be fun." What is being suggested here is that the students learn the material for their standardized exams within the authentic learning framework. For teachers, the scariest thing about this is feeling a loss of control: "If I am not lecturing and asking the questions (recitation style), how can I be sure that the students will learn the factual material for the exams?"

If you are lecturing and asking the questions, how can you be sure that the students are learning the material? What actually happens is that although teachers are sure that they are covering the material, they have little idea what students are actually learning. Beyond that is the issue of what we mean by the term "learning?" Is learning the ability to answer a test question and then forget the material the next day or week? Or, is learning understanding and being able to utilize the information in the future?

Many standardized state exams are essentially reading tests that appear to test factual content. When the answer choices are examined, students with good test taking skills can often figure out the correct answer, even if they have not memorized the specific factual content in the question. If the students are working with the skills and concepts of social studies, then most of the time they should be able to reason out the correct answers given that they will be using the factual content of the course during their authentic learning projects.

As long as teachers include some instruction on taking multiple-choice and/or traditional essay exams, and some practice opportunities across the school term, there is no reason to believe that teachers cannot use authentic learning strategies and have students who can pass high-stakes tests. In fact, it may surprise you that students might actually do better on the standardized tests because they have learned, as opposed to memorized, course content. That kind of outcome—students receiving higher grades on the state exam—was recently reported by a teacher during an NCSS annual meeting session.

## How Can I Be Sure My Students Are Really Learning the Content if I Don't Lecture and Assign Worksheets or Chapter Questions?

As mentioned in the last section, how can you be sure anyway? Many students simply copy the answers to worksheets from one another or "pick out" the answers to chapter questions without ever reading the chapter. These student "strategies" do not ensure learning. The secret is well-designed projects and rubrics with criteria that assure the inclusion of pertinent factual material. You can direct the relevant state standards content to the "expert" groups in a cooperative learning jigsaw. Just be sure that the cooperative learning groups are well-balanced so that there are students in every group who can assure that the pertinent information is gathered. Or, provide an answer-key checklist of factual information for the expert groups to review prior to returning to their home groups to teach the information to their peers.

You will need to teach the students that they can learn from each other in addition to learning from the teacher. There are several ways to do this.

- Have each expert group prepare a quiz for the rest of the class.
- Prepare a teacher-made quiz or test based on the standards, and administer it at the end of the unit in place of the individual essay (or any individual component of the project) suggested in the example in Chapter 2. Over time, and with practice, students will adapt and take more responsibility for including the relevant material without the threat of a test.
- Another strategy is a teacher-led, end-of-project review day where the teacher uses a graphic organizer to condense the factual content that is most important.

To illustrate, we can return to the example in Chapter 2 on learning what is meant by the term "democratic government." You might design a chart for the overhead projector or the chalkboard with the class consensus of criteria for democracy on the left side of the chart and the columns for Athens, Sparta, etc., along the top (see Figure 3.1). The students and the teacher would fill in the chart together at the end of the unit, providing the teacher with "insurance" that the students have the relevant information in their notebooks. Then students would have this concise chart to study for the exit exam (final or state exam) at the end of the school term.

## Figure 3.1. Comparing and Contrasting Governments

|  | Athens | Sparta | Roman Republic | Roman Empire | United States |
|---|---|---|---|---|---|
| Citizenship |  |  |  |  |  |
| Voting |  |  |  |  |  |
| Legal System |  |  |  |  |  |
| Freedom of Speech |  |  |  |  |  |
| Freedom of Religion |  |  |  |  |  |
| Habeas Corpus |  |  |  |  |  |
| Etc. |  |  |  |  |  |

Other graphic organizers would work just as well. Using such organizational structures has the advantage of teaching students an additional study skill. By condensing large amounts of important material on a single page, the student will be able to make connections, see relationships, etc. One excellent source of graphic organizers is the *Inspiration* software or Web site (http://www.inspiration.com/).

## How Do I Adapt the Lessons/Units I Am Currently Using?

You may be thinking that if it took so long to put together my current curriculum plans, how easily can they be changed or adapted? The answer is that it depends on the plans. Remember, we are moving from teacher-centered to student-centered instruction. Thus, many current lesson plans will need alteration. I would stress that if you have well thought out goals and objectives/outcomes with knowledge, skills, and disposition (attitude) accounted for in your current lesson plans, those will rarely change. The instructional strategy or method of reaching these goals is what is changing. So, look through the suggested lessons in this book for plans that approximate your goals and objectives and try those first.

However, if your current goals and objectives, when reconsidered, don't focus on essential questions, skills, and attitudes, they need some alteration anyway. Often as teachers, we become wedded to a lesson or activity that "worked" because the kids enjoyed it. Then, upon further reflection, we realize that the activity was fun but not relevant to either our old goals or our new ones. Time is short and content is ever increasing. Teachers must be prepared to let go of activities that are fun but do not fit into the curriculum in a meaningful way.

Although authentic learning does emphasize depth over breadth, the lessons in this book include examples that try to cover breadth (for standards-based curriculum) as well. If your current lessons do not meet the students' needs, they must be changed. Remember, do not throw away the whole course. Phase in the new lessons where the old ones are the least adaptable and keep revising every semester or year. Do not try to do more than you are comfortable with in any one term. The only problem you may have is when the students really begin to enjoy authentic instruction: they may push to come up with more projects and less traditional teaching!

## I Am Still Worried about My Students' Willingness to Do This Much Work

Once you get the projects fine-tuned, they should run like a well-oiled machine. The machine does the work while you steer and stay alert for "abnormal engine sounds." Occasionally, you will need to perform routine maintenance. Part of this maintenance is pacing. You need to continually adjust the amount of time that students are given to complete lessons to a pace where students are able to successfully finish the task but do not have time to waste because they finished earlier than the other groups. This is hard to do the first time a project/unit is taught, but becomes easier to judge with practice.

Students will stay on task and do the work if they see the value behind it. People rise to the level of your expectations. It is up to you, the teacher, to design projects that interest students and are relevant to real-world concerns. It is up to you to work with the media resource people and librarians to be sure that the resources and technology that will be needed are available. And, it is up to you to ensure that students will know how to access and use these resources, as well as how to work effectively in groups.

Thus, you may find yourself teaching teamwork, group process, etc. in the beginning of the year. If you are a coach, this is the chance to put some of those coaching skills to work in your teaching!

## My Technology Skills Are Weak. How Will I Integrate Technology into the Lessons?

If your technology skills are weak and you want to have students use presentation software, think about in-service or faculty development opportunities in that area. Further, as states implement technology standards for K–12 students and their teachers, many students will come to class already having developed excellent technology skills. Have these students teach you what you need to know about technology. Students will enjoy this opportunity to "teach the teacher" and you will benefit from the instruction. This models for students that you are not the giver of all wisdom, but that you are a learner just like they are.

This is a good time to remind you that the Internet links in the lesson plans will need to be checked before teaching each lesson. Although I have tried to select Web sites that are stable, the Web is dynamic, and organizations do change servers, Web-space providers, etc. Also, some of the URLs in the lessons are quite long, and students might make errors typing them into the browser. A suggestion to help with this problem is that if your school provides you with a teacher Web site, it might be easier to transfer the links used in the lessons to your home page to make student connections easier, faster, and more precise. Or, Teacher Web, (http\\www.teacherweb.com) provides free Web sites on which teachers can post information and hyperlinks.

## How Will My Special Needs Students Complete These Projects?

With most schools around the country moving away from tracking, as well as moving toward either mainstreaming or full inclusion for special education students, teachers need new strategies for differentiating instruction. One of the best things about authentic learning and assessment is how much easier this is to accomplish within this framework.

First, when it comes to research and finding materials, all students will not be confined to the same textbook or feel a "stigma" if they need easier materials to read. You can keep a variety of different levels of text-based resources in your room, especially those labeled "high interest, low reading level."

In addition, by using computer and video resources, special education students might be able to locate the information that will enable them to contribute to the group work in ways they previously could not have achieved in traditional classrooms. If possible, work with assistance from the special education teachers to design inclusive authentic projects that their mainstreamed students can handle.

Lastly, as the teacher, you have now become the facilitator, so you will have more time to spend assisting these individual students while the others move along on their independent or group work. Because the assignments are connected to the real world, the abstract nature of some social studies content is contained in a more meaningful context, thus helping students who might not have been successful in traditional classrooms reach understandings that might have eluded them before.

Thus, using authentic, performance-based tasks and rubrics will assist teachers in dealing with the range of students in their classes by helping differentiate instruction within the project assignment, rather than viewing the move toward inclusion as "just another burden for the teacher."

## How Can I Be Confident That My Grading Is Fair (Valid and Reliable)?

Any time a teacher switches to a new grading system, the problem is similar. How sure are you now that your assessments are valid and reliable? Think back to your old "tests and measurements" course, if you had one, and try to remember all the types of validity that you studied: content validity, criterion validity, face validity, etc.

How do you defend your present grading system to colleagues, the administration, students and/or parents? Now think about the earlier discussion on curriculum alignment. Begin with goals and outcomes. Design a project that meets those goals and outcomes. Then, design a rubric for grading that incorporates the factors necessary for students to achieve those goals and outcome. How can anyone question the fairness and validity of the grades when they have been derived in this fashion?

Remember, you may be incorporating the national, state, or local curriculum standards into your goals and objectives/outcomes. Because you are usually distributing the grading rubric on the same day that you assign the project tasks, the students will know what is expected from the beginning of each task. Nothing can be more fair than that!

A word of caution is in order here. When grading an essay, even when using a point system like the one used in the example within Figure 2.1, it takes time to learn to be consistent, the hallmark of reliability. This is true with traditional essay tests as well as authentic essay questions. The difference is simply the type of question asked.

Begin by reading through all the papers and dividing them into tentative piles of excellent, very good, satisfactory, and unacceptable. Then, try to assess the criteria that made you select a particular pile for any given essay. After a list of criteria has been compiled, pick an "average" essay from each pile and use that as a "benchmark." These essay answers become the benchmarks for "A," "B," "C," "D," and "F."

Without reviewing the name of the student, you can show these essays as examples of what performance quality you expect. To do this fairly, you need to type these essays in order to mask a student's handwriting. Then, to review the essays with the class, copy them onto an overhead transparency, or provide another way for the class to see them.

You need to share the list of established criteria with the class. Have the students read the sample essays and point out where the criteria were, or were not, met. You can even include a list of potential factual data for the question. This takes a subjective question, the essay, and makes the grading more objective as students see what factual evidence is expected in an essay answer.

"Whoa, you say. "This is a lot of work!" Yes, but there are shortcuts. Sometimes you can find lesson examples with essays similar to what you would like to use that come with criteria lists and examples. For advanced classes, it is fairly easy to obtain examples of Advanced Placement essays that include both factual material and scoring rubrics. Another shortcut would be to begin by assigning a short essay; for instance, ask for one-paragraph answers, rather than five paragraphs. You will get the hang of it. Besides, the criteria lists for writing essays are fairly consistent:

For example, for an A:

- The essay contains a well-developed topic (thesis) sentence that focuses on the question asked;
- Social studies terms were defined clearly;
- Three examples (however many required) were provided;
- Two facts (however many required) backed up each example;
- The conclusion supports the factual evidence;
- There were few or no factual errors; and

♦ Essay was well written, spelling and grammar correct.

For a B:
♦ The topic sentence simply restates the question;
♦ Two examples were provided;
♦ One fact backed up each example;
♦ The conclusion is not completely backed up by the evidence presented;
♦ There were minor errors; and
♦ The writing was good, minor grammar or spelling errors.

Once you have completed this process a few times, you will become very quick at establishing an essay checklist and applying it reliably. Many teachers use a "generic" grading list. Then, with that list established, all that you do is draw up a list of the pertinent factual information needed to competently answer the specific question being asked.

Another suggestion is to grade the essays before looking at the student's name to focus on the quality of the work. This prevents bias because it eliminates your preconceived notion of any student's ability. Later, you can adjust the grade for a special needs student, etc. This is most easily accomplished by having students write their names on the back, rather than the front, of the essay paper. Then, you will not see the name prior to grading.

Practice with establishing essay criteria and benchmarks with examples helps you move from the type of scoring rubric used in Figure 2.1, with its point value assessments, to more holistic, open-ended assessments, while still reassuring students that they are being treated fairly. Over time, students should become familiar enough with applying these rubrics that if a batch of essay answers were typed up (anonymously), the students would be able to grade them fairly accurately.

I am not suggesting that your students grade each other's papers! I am suggesting that teachers will learn to be specific enough in their requirements so that the students will understand what is expected of them. In terms of receiving any specific grade, everyone will feel comfortable with fairly grading subjective work, including nonessay, performance-based work. Of course, with consistent expectations, you would not be supplying the grading rubric for each essay in advance. The general format used in the example above could be posted in the classroom as a guideline for all essays throughout the school term.

Although extended written work is a criterion that both Wiggins and Newmann believe is required for true authentic instruction, not all projects will have essay work assigned, or even large amounts of written work, for teachers to grade. Frequently, students will participate in oral communication assignments such as debates, role-playing, or simulations. Sometimes, multimedia presentations will be the end product. All of these assignments will be graded as they occur in the classroom. No matter what performance or product the teacher assigns, all of these will need clear, consistent rubrics with benchmarks in order for them to be graded fairly.

How much time is currently spent writing traditional test questions or creating tests from prewritten test banks supplied with the textbook? How many times have students argued that a multiple-choice, true-false, or short-answer question was unfair for any number of reasons? How often have you discarded the question because it was poorly worded, misleading, or just a bad question? Because every teacher and every class is a little different, it is very difficult to use the same standardized test for every class you teach—it is even harder to defend that practice to the administration and the parents. All that is happening with authentic assessment is that you are spending your time differently. You are thinking about your goals and objectives and how to assess them in a different format. In the following chapters, there are examples to get you started. Once you become familiar with the format and requirements, you will be able to plan authentic lessons and units as easily as you did the traditional lessons and tests.

# 4
# Social Studies Themes

This chapter is comprised of lesson plan suggestions with accompanying grading rubrics. The lessons have been designed to meet the criteria for authentic instruction (learning and assessment) within the framework of the curriculum standards suggested by the National Council for the Social Studies (NCSS). The NCSS standards, *Expectations of Excellence: Curriculum Standards for Social Studies*, are being used because they favor interdisciplinary or multidisciplinary approaches to the social studies/history curriculum.

Each section defines and briefly discusses one NCSS curriculum standard and then provides two lesson examples appropriate for social studies classrooms grades 9 through 12. The lesson plan examples include topics from civics, government, economics, world history, United States history, world regions or cultures, and geography—the subject areas most commonly covered in our public schools. However, the main focus is world history and U.S. history, because those subjects are required in almost all school districts.

Although not every section has an example for every subject area, many of the social studies themes overlap by topic or academic content. Accordingly, the lessons or strategies may be useful regardless of the particular course to which the lesson has been assigned. If you are looking for a particular history topic, be sure to check the civics or geography lessons to see if you can adapt one of the lesson suggestions. Remember, the key to success is your flexibility. The lessons presented have often been chosen because they are adaptable. Bruner (1960) tells us that we can teach anything to anybody at some level of specificity—so feel free to adapt a lesson to middle school from the high school level suggested, and vice versa.

One of the main purposes of this book, besides providing specific lesson examples, is to stimulate ideas for you to develop on your own. Use these lessons both as presented and as starting points to create your own ideas and lessons. Borrow ideas for grading rubrics from one lesson to use with another if it better suits your class or meets your students' needs.

In addition to providing lesson examples from the range of social studies courses commonly taught, the lessons are heavily technology based. The purpose is to assist teachers in incorporating technology into their teaching in a meaningful way. Because many of the newer technology resources are Internet-based, rather than software- based, the focus is on Internet or Web-based lessons.

If your particular school does not have the suggested technology resources, be flexible. Think about how you could accomplish similar goals without the technology. If you don't have the Internet in the classroom, bring the Internet to the students. Often this means:

Going to the library or media center. Accessing the Web sites suggested. Downloading the information on the Web site. Printing the information. Making copies of the printouts for students to share in the classroom.

Lessons from some chapters are geared towards either interdisciplinary or multidisciplinary cooperation among teachers. Remember, the purpose here is authentic learning and assessment with active students and teacher facilitators. Combining study across subjects helps students make connections and promotes deeper understandings. It is risky for teachers to reach across traditional department separations. Be brave. Try it.

Although bridging subjects may be difficult at first, the benefit to students is immense as they see their teachers modeling the same cooperative learning skills that they are being taught. Working with colleagues will also alert teachers to the difficulties students have working in groups. This might help teachers deal with interpersonal problems as they arise in the classroom.

The NCSS themes that form the framework of standards for the social studies are
- Culture
- Time, Continuity, and Change
- People, Places, and Environments
- Individual Development and Identity
- Individuals, Groups, and Institutions
- Power, Authority, and Governance
- Production, Distribution, and Consumption
- Science, Technology, and Society
- Global Connections
- Civic Ideals and Practices

Although the chapters are arranged by NCSS theme, the lessons incorporate the national standards in the appropriate subject area. Thus, lesson objectives list the objectives from publications including:
- *Voluntary National Content Standards in Economics*
- *National Standards for Civics and Government*
- *National Standards for History*
- *National Standards for World History*
- *Geography for Life*

This should enable teachers using a single subject rather than a social studies approach to adapt the lessons to their needs.

# Culture

The first social studies theme is culture. No history or social studies course can be effectively taught without addressing the concept of culture. The *Random House Dictionary* (1987) defines culture as " the behaviors and beliefs characteristic of a particular social, ethnic or age group." Or alternately, as "the quality in a person or society that arises from a concern for what is regarded as excellent in arts, letters, manners, scholarly pursuits, etc." Thus, teachers can approach the theme of culture from at least two angles. First, culture as the traditional cultural geography or study of early civilizations, anthropology, or sociology study within social studies/history. Or second, culture in combination with humanities, English, music, or art as a study of the intellectual products of humans.

The understandings about culture that students need include:
- Recognition of common characteristics of different cultures.
- Relationship of cultural belief systems to economic and political aspects of a society.
- Relationship of intellectual products of a culture to the beliefs of the members of that culture. These include:
  - Art
  - Music
  - Architecture
  - Literature

The United States history lesson for this standard is entitled "Regional Differences." The lesson takes a traditional topic of study, colonial America, and provides the teacher with an opportunity to experiment with the use of learning centers at the high school level. This is a particularly good lesson for practice with learning centers because most of the students will have some familiarity with the topic of colonial America from earlier grades. Thus, the teacher can focus on the process of learning centers as well as the historic content while allowing each student to work at his or her own level.

Although the directions may appear complex, remember that learning centers have long been used in elementary schools and, sometimes, middle schools. The increasing diversity of our high school classrooms makes the establishment of learning centers an attractive option for high school teachers who need to differentiate instruction and still ensure that the standards in their state curriculum are addressed for each student

Although the setup of the lesson is time-consuming, the teacher will find that the day-to-day teaching of the content will be less stressful (George, McEwin, & Jenkins, 2000, p. 97). Because the topic of colonial America falls early in the school year, teachers have the opportunity to use this lesson to get to know their students individually. Thus, teachers can learn about their students—their strengths and weaknesses, motivation, etc.—at the outset of the school term. Using learning centers at this early point in the year teaches students to become responsible, active learners. In addition, using learning centers prepares students for other cooperative learning and group projects that will occur across the school year.

After reading over the lesson, you might wonder: what makes this lesson an authentic learning experience when it appears to have few "real-world" connections? Although the content does not have real-world connection, the process of using learning centers teaches the following:

- Students have been placed in the center of their own learning based on their prior knowledge (from the pretest).
- Students are working at becoming independent people who can be assigned a challenging task and complete it in a timely manner.
- Students are learning to ask for help only when they truly need assistance.

These are skills necessary for success in the adult world as defined by the SCANS report discussed in earlier chapters. In addition, these skills help students to become the life-long learners required by *Goals 2000*. The lesson, designed for early in the school year, serves as a bridge from traditional social studies/history class to authentic instruction by maintaining a focus on traditional academic content, but altering the process of obtaining the information.

The second lesson in the chapter, "Coping with Change: The Rise of Modern Europe," addresses world history curriculum. This time period, encompassing the decline of feudalism and the rise of the monarchies, is often difficult to teach because the textbook chapters tend to have separate sections for each nation covered by the time period. Thus, the traditional approach to this topic has teachers lecturing on England on Monday, France on Tuesday, Germany on Wednesday, etc. This is generally boring, trivial, and meaningless to students.

The approach suggested by the lesson is to use cooperative learning groups to cover the material by assigning each group to a different nation. The groups will present the required social studies content to the class. The groups can subdivide using the PERSIA organizer discussed in Chapter 1. In that way, each student is accountable for his or her portion and presentation of one aspect (political, economic, religious, social, intellectual, or aesthetic) for one country. The entire group is responsible for presenting all the necessary historic content for that country. If students are required to take notes during the group presentations, then all students will have the information for all countries covered in the chapter and be prepared to study for a test on the material. Thus, each student attains both the depth of knowledge in one area as well as the breadth required by the curriculum standards. It is the depth that helps make the material understandable and meaningful.

As in the U.S. history lesson, the real-world connection is focused more on process skills than academic content. Students learn:

- Working with others to complete a task.
- Individual accountability for a specific portion of the task.
- Accessing information.
- Separating important from unimportant information.
- Communication and presentation skills.
- Evaluation of self, group, and presentations.

This basic lesson format works at any point in the curriculum where the textbook chapter focuses on a general theme and each chapter section within that chapter addresses that theme in a different country or world region. Thus, if the teacher wanted to introduce cooperative learning at the beginning of the term, the model could be used during the first weeks of school when students begin to study the unit on the four river-valley civilizations (Egypt, Mesopotamia, India, and China). Each cooperative group is assigned a different civilization. The PERSIA information is gathered as explained above.

For a shorter exercise designed to introduce both the process of cooperative learning and to cover a lot of material quickly, the teacher might simply choose the Mesopotamian civilizations mentioned in the textbook. By using smaller groups (two or three per student group), the teacher could assign: Sumerians, Assyrians, Babylonians, Chaldeans, Hittites, Akkadians, Lydians, Phoenicians, Hebrews, etc. Students could complete a chart during the oral presentations that would highlight the important points about each civilization. The chart or graphic organizer would help students as a study skills tool early in the school year while students are grappling with how to master the overwhelming amount of information included in a standard world history course curriculum.

It is important to note that these lessons could be reversed. The U.S. history teachers can use cooperative learning to teach regional development in colonial America by assigning one group to each region. The only problem would be to keep groups no larger than five students per group. Or, the world history teachers could create learning centers for each country in Western Europe covered in the cooperative group project lesson. What is important is that teachers modify the lessons to fit their curriculum and practice both of these instructional strategies when the historical material is appropriate.

# The Regional Differences in American History

## NCSS Theme
### Culture

"Apply an understanding of culture as an integrated whole that explains the functions and interactions of language, literature, the arts, traditions, beliefs and values, and behavior patterns." [a]

"Compare and analyze societal patterns for preserving and transmitting culture while adapting to environmental or social change." [a]

## Objectives
### Subject Area National Standards

United States History: "Era 2: colonization and settlement (1585-1763)." [b]

Standard 1A: "The student understands how diverse immigrants affected the formation of European colonies in North America." [b]

Standard 2A: "How political, religious and social institutions emerged in the English colonies." [c]

Standard 2B: "The student understands religious diversity in the colonies and how ideas about religious freedom evolved." [c]

Standard 3A: "The student understands colonial economic life and labor systems in the Americas." [d]

### Skills Standards or Objectives

Era 2, Standard 1A: "The student is able to compare the social composition of English, French, and Dutch settlers in the 17th and 18th centuries (interrogate historic data)." [b]

Standard 1B: "The student is able to compare how English settlers interacted with Native Americans in New England, mid-Atlantic, Chesapeake, and lower South colonies." [b]

Standard 3A: "The student is able to identify the major economic regions in the Americas and explain how labor systems shaped them (utilize visual and mathematical data)." [d]

Standard 3B: "The student is able to understand how environmental and human factors accounted for differences in the economies that developed in the colonies of New England, mid-Atlantic, Chesapeake, and lower South (compare and contrast)." [d]

### Attitude Standards or Objectives

Students will appreciate both the differences (diversity) and the similarities (commonalities) in American life and culture.

Students will understand the importance of becoming active learners responsible for mastering required course content.

Students will learn to share resources, manage time efficiently, work independently and follow directions.

[a] *Expectations of Excellence*, p.111
[b] *National Standards for World History*, p. 81
[c] p. 82
[d] p. 83

# Culture

## Procedures

### Set

The focus of this section of the lesson is preparing the class for independent learning through the use of learning centers (stations).

- The teacher needs to arrange the classroom with five or six learning centers prior to students entering the classroom.
- The centers might be groups of desks or preferably tables with chairs clustered in the corners and perhaps the middle of the room.
- Groups of students need room to cluster at each center as well as to move freely among the centers as they complete their work.
- Each center needs to be labeled. For this lesson, there needs to be at least one center each for:
  - New England colonies.
  - Mid-Atlantic colonies.
  - Chesapeake colonies.
  - Lower South colonies.
  - Additionally, there might be a center for earlier immigration (English, Dutch, and French colonies) that serves as a review.
- There should be several activities (at least five) for students to complete at each station.
  - One easy way to set this up the first time might be to divide the learning objectives at each center into political, social, economic, religious, and cultural categories by setting up an activity that addresses each.
  - Another approach would be to have different media at each station (small TV with VTR or filmstrip player with filmstrip, computer with CD-ROM, or laser disk player with information.
  - A source for setting up centers is Jackdaw kits. These are relatively inexpensive ($40/kit) and include primary source documents, pictures, etc. that can be used as the core of the center.
- A handout or learning guide needs to be prepared for each student with the instructions for completing the lesson. This would include:
  - The number of class periods (days) the student has to complete the work.
  - The instructions for obtaining and completing the work at each center (or station).
  - Procedures for submitting work and moving to the next center.
  - A grading or evaluation rubric.
- If this is a first time using learning centers, teachers might preassign students to a starting center to avoid crowding at any one station. Or, using the seating of the traditional class, row one might start at New England, row two at mid-Atlantic, etc.

- Teachers have a choice of either handing out all the questions to be completed on this guide, or, especially for a less motivated class, the question sheet for each center can be located in a folder at that center. In this way, the amount of work assigned will not seem as overwhelming because students will address each center and its work in a piecemeal fashion.
- Teachers have the option of using a traditional pre-test to prepare students.
- Each student would use the centers either to remediate or to enrich his or her knowledge based on the pre-test grade obtained.
- The question sheets accompanying the activities at each station could include a series of questions. Rather than each student completing every question, the teacher might instruct each student which questions to complete based on the pre-test.

## *Body of Lesson*

- Students work independently at each center completing the assignment or question sheet appropriate at each station.
- As students finish their activities at one center they submit their completed question sheet.
- Students may not move to the next station without teacher permission signifying that their work has been satisfactory.
- Teachers monitor the centers, conference with students and assist as needed.
- Teachers must constantly circulate to ensure that all students are engaged and actively on task doing their own work.

## *Closure*

- There should be a traditional post-test covering the standards and objectives for the lesson (unit).
- In addition, students should write an essay (this could be open-note to add an incentive to complete the question sheet) comparing and contrasting the regions of colonial settlement.
- If there is time, or for enrichment, students might explore whether or not there are still regional differences in America today.
  - If so, what regions would they locate (would they add the Southwest, the Northwest, or the Far West)?
  - What do we, as Americans, have in common? Are today's mass media uniting or dividing us?
  - If there are a number of advanced students in the class, this section could become an additional center or station.
  - Perhaps, if they have done exceptionally well on the pre-test, these students might create this station in lieu of the regular class assignment.

# Culture

## Timing

Given the amount of preparation, this lesson really serves as a unit rather than a single lesson. Research states that a learning center assignment should take no less than one school week to make the planning and setup worth the teacher's time, and no more than two weeks because students lose motivation after that time. Alterations should be made for block scheduling.

## Materials

- Teachers need to collect materials from various sources to create learning stations or centers.
  - As mentioned earlier, the Jackdaw kits make a nice foundation for learning centers. These and other materials are available from the Social Studies School Service Catalogue or on line at: http://socialstudies.com/c/@sIzMgrvUMu80o/Pages/index.html
  - The American Memory Web site at the Library of Congress, http://memory.loc.gov/, is an excellent source of documents, pictures, and music in American History.
  - The Smithsonian National American History Museum, http://americanhistory.si.edu/, is another source for materials.
  - The National Archives, http://www.nara.gov/exhall/exhibits.html has online exhibits to access.
  - Additional Web sites with Colonial information, maps, documents, etc., include:
    - http://falcon.jmu.edu/~ramseyil/colonial.htm
    - Colonial New England: http://www.glasgow-ky.com/fye/ms_fye/colonial_life.htm
    - http://www.7cs.com/collectibles.colonial.html
    - http://www.d300.kane.k12.il.us/SchoolSites/lith/pages/g5/colonial.htm
    - http://www.gryphonbooksforwriters.com/Colonial.htm
    - http://www.e-connections.org/lesson1/Tlesson1.htm
    - http://www.sodamnhip.com/colammid.html
    - http://odur.let.rug.nl/~usa/H/1994/chap2.htm
    - http://www.concord.k12.nh.us/schools/kimball/classes/mitchell/colonial.htm
- The key to successful learning centers is to have different activities at varied academic levels at each station. This could include high-interest, low-level literature if the teacher wanted to integrate literature into an interdisciplinary unit.
- Each station should include:
  - Map work
  - Document analysis from first-person accounts of settlement

- Pictures or artwork
- If computers are available, colonial Web sites can be bookmarked or listed on the teacher's home page. For example:
    - Jamestown, http://www.iath.virginia.edu/vcdh/jamestown/.
    - Colonial Williamsburg, http://www.history.org/history/.
    - Mt Vernon, http://www.mountvernon.org/
    - Monticello, http://www.monticello.org/
    - Sturbridge Village, http://www.osv.org

Remember, after the unit is completed, dismantle the stations by organizing a file for each region. Box and label each center's materials for use the following year. Each year, add one new choice of activity for each center.

Over time, the learning center approach enables a truly differentiated curricular activity to address the needs of all students in the classroom.

The suggested scoring rubric contains both content and behavior areas for the awarding of points. Teachers will need to determine the number of points they wish to award for the total assignment. Then divide as appropriate. There is an extra credit option that may or may not be utilized—it is up to the teacher. At the bottom of the rubric, teachers may insert a key to convert points to letter grades when necessary.

Culture

# Evaluation Rubric

| Points Earned | Points Possible | |
|---|---|---|
| | | **Pre-Test Grade** |
| | | **Questions assigned and completed** (full sentences, correct anwer) |
| | | * Early Colonies |
| | | * New England |
| | | * Mid-Atlantic |
| | | * Chesapeake |
| | | * Lower South |
| | | **Post-Test Grade** |
| | | **Essay Question** |
| | | * Thesis or topic sentence |
| | | * Compared colonial regions |
| | | * Contrasted colonial regions |
| | | * Used examples of: |
| | | ¤ Political |
| | | ¤ Social |
| | | ¤ Economic |
| | | ¤ Religious |
| | | ¤ Cultural |
| | | * Writing Style |
| | | ¤ Grammar |
| | | ¤ Spelling |
| | | **Work Habits** |
| | | * Followed directions |
| | | * Stayed on task |
| | | * Worked independently |
| | | * Shared center resources |
| | | * Assisted classmates when asked for help |
| | | **Extra Credit** contributed additional resource materials for the learning center |
| | | **Total** |
| **Key** | A= B= C= D= E= F= | |
| **Comments:** | | |

# Coping with Change:
# The Rise of Modern Europe

## NCSS Theme
### Culture

"Analyze the ways groups, societies, and cultures address human needs and concerns."[a]

"Apply an understanding of culture as an integrated whole that explains the functions and interactions of language, literature, the arts, traditions, beliefs and values, and behavior patterns."[a]

## Objectives
### Subject Area National Standards

World History Era 5
Standard 2: "The redefining of European society and culture, 1000–1300 C.E."[b]
Standard 2A: "Students should be able to 'demonstrates the understanding of feudalism and the growth of centralized monarchies and city-states in Europe...'"[b]

### Skills Standard or Objective

"...[analyze] how European monarchies expanded their power at the expense of feudal lords and assess the growth and limitations of representative institutions in these monarchies [analyze cause and effect]."

### Attitude Standards or Objectives

Students will be able to work cooperatively with others.
Students will appreciate the difficulties of life in times of change.
Students will appreciate the cultures that developed in Western Europe in this time period.

[a] *Expectations of Excellence*, p. 111
[b] *National Standards for World History*, p. 140

## Procedures
### Set

Review with students the reasons for the decline of feudalism and the rise of towns and cities from their previous studies.

- Ask students what kind of governments they imagine will form at this point.
- Why do they think that? (Expect answers based on old movies and/or stories.) The teacher can mention specific movies or stories to give students a hint that there will be new countries formed with kings or monarchs as leaders.

Culture 49

## *Body of Lesson*

Explain to students the next topic of study in their textbook is concerned with the "Rise of Monarchies in Europe."

- This includes the countries of Spain, France, England, Germany, and Russia.
- The purpose of our project is to learn about the people and their governments in a historic period when Western Europe was undergoing the change from feudalism to modern times. We study this to help understand why these countries have developed and become the way they are today.

For this assignment the class will be divided into teacher-selected cooperative groups.

- Each group will be assigned one or more of the above countries.
- The assignments are based on the chapter sections in the textbook and the amount of resource material available in the school library/media center.
- There will be *no* shifting of groups or assignments.
- Each group will select one student as its leader.
- The leader will receive extra credit for the additional responsibility.

Procedure: The ground rules need to be very clearly spelled out for students. Starting with the bulleted information, a handout can be given to the students with the following information:

- Groups will be assigned on Monday. Each group must select a leader and submit that name to the teacher.
- On Monday and Tuesday class will meet in the school library/media center to give groups a chance to organize and prepare their presentations.
- Oral reports will be presented on the following Monday.
  - Each group will have 25 minutes or approximately three to five minutes per student.
  - We will have five presentations in three days, so adherence to time limitations will be part of your grade.
- Groups will be prepared by Thursday and will be selected by lottery for their presentation order.
  - Completed group folders are to be handed in on Friday.
- Requirements for reports:
  - Each student is responsible for an oral presentation and for a short, written report that the presentation was based upon.
  - These reports are to be collected in a folder with the name of the group assignment and members on the front of the folder.
  - All reports are to be *typed, double spaced*
  - The report must include an accurate bibliography in proper format (MLA or MacMillan 10).
  - Each student must use at least three sources with no more than one encyclopedia and no more than one textbook.

- Magazines
- Vertical files
- Resource books (should be available in the library and in the resource area of our classroom)
- Computer information resources (available in the library and the classroom)

The information presented in these reports will vary for each group because the assigned topics will vary. Part of each student's grade will be determined by the decisions the group makes about material to include, style and order of presentation, decisions to use visual aids, handouts for the class, etc. The group reports should include:

- Introduction
- Information about geographical location
- Political structure of the country
- Economic information
- Social information
- Intellectual life of the areas covered
- A conclusion

Interesting stories, illustrations, or other aids will make presentations more fun.
The purpose of the project is educational, but there is room here for creativity. Remember class, you are both presenters and audience. We would like to have an enjoyable two days of presentations. Bear that in mind when you write your reports.
Each group must prepare a class handout that will serve as chapter notes for their section. If groups wish to have notes copied for handing out in class, the teacher must have the material by Wednesday. All handouts are to be included in student's World History notebooks.

## *Evaluation*

Grades will be determined by a combination of the following assessments:

- An evaluation of the group from the members of each group; an evaluation by the class of the group's presentation. (Although this may seem like a lot of evaluation paperwork, the self and group evaluation forms students complete on one another help students to stay on task and teach them self-assessment skills).
- An evaluation by the teacher of
  - Library work
  - Individual oral report
  - Group oral report,
  - Individual and group written report
  - Individual behavior during presentations.
- Students will receive a letter grade deduction from their project if the teacher needs to reprimand them during a classmate's presentations.

- The final grade for this project will count as 20 percent of the report card grade for the grading period.
- If a student is absent on the day his or her group presents, the group leader will be responsible for reading the report. If the leader does not have this report, the absent student will receive a 0 (zero) on this project!

At the end of the project, the teacher should receive from each student:
- A written report in the group folder
- A group evaluation sheet
- A self-evaluation
- A group presentation evaluation sheet.

If any one of these is missing or incomplete, there will be a grade deduction.

The historic period required includes tracing the development of the country from the barbarians and the fall of Rome (circa 500 C.E.) until the time period completed in the textbook chapter:
- England—1600s and the death of Elizabeth I
- France—the ascension of Louis XV in 1715
- Spain—1700s and the death of Charles II
- Germany (and Austria)—1763 Treaty of Paris
- Russia—1800 and the death of Catherine the Great

Include political, social, economic, religious, and intellectual materials for each country.

The groups need to understand and explain to the class why these countries and times were important!

There will be a test on all the material in the chapter following the presentations

## *Closure*

The closure is in two parts; the oral presentations and the chapter test. The test should have both traditional multiple-choice questions as well as an essay asking students to demonstrate their understanding of how European culture changed with the end of feudalism.

## Timing

Students will need two days for library research; one (or more) day(s) for group work in class to complete reports; three (or fewer) days for presentations, depending on the time the teacher chooses to allot for each group; and one day for a review and a short test.

## Materials

- Textbook
- Library resources or classroom resources (cart from library with books on topics).
- Internet sources for the teacher

- http://www.bridge-rayn.org/modern.html
- http://twist.lib.uiowa.edu/emsurvey/resources.html
- http://www2.sunysuffolk.edu/westn/modernroots.html
- http://www2.sunysuffolk.edu/westn/easteur.html#Russia
- http://www.britannica.com/eb/article?eu=109530&tocid=27689
- http://www.azstarnet.com/~qpriest/Courses/WC/McKay%20Chpts/Ch_16_Age_of_Monarchs.htm
- http://www.royalty.nu/Europe/index.html

Culture

# Student Self Evaluation Form

Name: _____

I think I deserve a grade of _____ on my oral project because:


I think I deserve a grade of _____ on my written project because:


# Presentation Evaluation

Base your decision about your group on the following information:
- Introduction was interesting and clear.
- Student report was concise, informative, and clear.
- Factual content was high.
- You learned something.
- Summary was interesting, concise, and clear.

You may rate either the group as a whole or single out any particular individual student/s in this section.

Group 1 deserves a grade of _____ because:


Group 2 deserves a grade of _____ because:


Group 3 deserves a grade of _____ because:


Group 4 deserves a grade of _____ because:


Group 5 deserves a grade of _____ because:


Student Name: _____

## Group Evaluation Form

Group Number _____

Group Members _____
_____
_____
_____
_____

This group was effective/ineffective because:


Who was the most influential group member?


Did any group member arouse antagonistic feelings? _____ Who?


Did the leader make sure that everyone's ideas were considered courteously?


Did all group members cooperate or did several do all the work?


Was the situation friendly/tense?


Do you have any suggestions for future group work?

# Evaluation Rubric
## Group Evaluation Summary Sheet

|     |                           | Germany | France | England | Russia | Spain |
|-----|---------------------------|---------|--------|---------|--------|-------|
| 50  | **Presentation**          |         |        |         |        |       |
| 5   | Intro/background          |         |        |         |        |       |
| 5   | Geography                 |         |        |         |        |       |
| 5   | Political                 |         |        |         |        |       |
| 5   | Economic                  |         |        |         |        |       |
| 5   | Religious                 |         |        |         |        |       |
| 5   | Social                    |         |        |         |        |       |
| 5   | Intellectual              |         |        |         |        |       |
| 5   | Aesthetic                 |         |        |         |        |       |
| 5   | Conclusion                |         |        |         |        |       |
| 5   | Time period covered       |         |        |         |        |       |
|     | Subtotal                  |         |        |         |        |       |
| 50  | **Form**                  |         |        |         |        |       |
| 5   | Clear and audible         |         |        |         |        |       |
| 5   | Eye contact               |         |        |         |        |       |
| 5   | Poise/confidence          |         |        |         |        |       |
| 5   | Includes all group members|         |        |         |        |       |
| 15  | Creative/format/interest  |         |        |         |        |       |
| 5   | Visuals                   |         |        |         |        |       |
| 10  | Handouts for class        |         |        |         |        |       |
|     | Subtotal                  |         |        |         |        |       |
| 20  | **Written**               |         |        |         |        |       |
| 1   | Folder                    |         |        |         |        |       |
| 2   | Names of group            |         |        |         |        |       |
| 1   | Cover                     |         |        |         |        |       |
| 2   | Organization of all reports|        |        |         |        |       |
| 2   | Copy of note handouts     |         |        |         |        |       |
|     | Bibliography              |         |        |         |        |       |
| 3   | Number of sources         |         |        |         |        |       |
| 2   | Variety of sources        |         |        |         |        |       |
| 2   | Format                    |         |        |         |        |       |
| 3   | Typed                     |         |        |         |        |       |
| 2   | Proofread                 |         |        |         |        |       |
|     | Subtotal                  |         |        |         |        |       |
| 30  | **Individual Contributions**|       |        |         |        |       |
| 10  | Behavior (library/class)  |         |        |         |        |       |
| 5   | Report and notes          |         |        |         |        |       |
| 5   | Research                  |         |        |         |        |       |
| 5   | Participation             |         |        |         |        |       |
| 5   | Evaluation forms completed|         |        |         |        |       |
|     | Subtotal                  |         |        |         |        |       |
|     | Total                     |         |        |         |        |       |

# Time, Continuity, and Change

The theme of time, continuity, and change helps students to understand how to locate themselves in time and place. Whether the teacher seeks to show that the past can have elements of recurring patterns or to demonstrate that old solutions might not work for new problems, students need to struggle with the past in order to understand the present and to prepare for the future. How do things change over time? What remains the same? What is completely different? How can we link the past and the present? How can we accept change as an inevitable part of human experience? How can we become comfortable with change in our lives?

Although this theme is most applicable to history courses, there is room for the teacher to develop basic geographic understandings as demonstrated by the map lesson. Additionally, the theme can be used to develop economic and political insights as a student grapples with human chronology. A multidisciplinary approach might allow teachers in several academic disciplines (science, math, and English) to focus on the theme of "time," "continuity," or "change" in order to provide students with a more in-depth understanding of these concepts. This focus would not require that all teachers study the same concept at the same time. Perhaps colleagues across departments might want to select one of these words and explore it within the context of their subject area.

The first lesson in this section, "Understanding Maps," uses world history information that can be easily adapted for U.S. history or geography. This lesson is concerned with teaching students how history is affected by geography. The first requirement for any historic study is to locate the topic or subject in time and place. This is accomplished by using historic maps and atlases. The teacher can use any historic era or location to design a map assignment that requires a student to struggle with how to communicate a large amount of information in the graphic form we call a "map." Thus, it is important that the teacher require more information than is currently available on a single map, thereby forcing students to consult several sources in order to complete the assignment.

For example, the teacher could select Native American Tribes for the mapping project. Students might have to map the locations, types of dwellings, crops grown, hunting grounds, tribal migrations, current reservation areas, etc. In addition, standard topographical and symbol information (directional symbol, scale, latitude and longitude) should be required. Students overwhelmed with how to display that much information on a single surface begin to understand map design as well as basic requirements for communicating information. The teacher can pose questions about the economic, social, and political inferences for students to answer from the maps they have designed. For students who are not used to studying maps, this might help them focus on the maps included in their textbooks instead of simply skipping to the next page of text.

The second lesson, "What If," can be used in U.S. history, world history, or geography. The ideas of time, continuity, and change are demonstrated by having students answer basic questions about life in a different place or time period. This lesson is keyed to basic historic understandings in the national history standards rather than focusing on a specific era or subject.

# Understanding Maps

## NCSS Theme

### Time, Continuity, and Change

"Identify and describe significant historic periods and patterns of change within and across cultures, such as the development of ancient cultures and civilizations, the rise of nation-states, and social, economic, and political revolutions."[a]

## Objectives

### Subject Area National Standard

Standard 2: Historical Comprehension—"Draw upon data in historic maps."[b]

### Skills Standard or Objective

Standard 4: Historical Research Capabilities. "Students will be able to: Identify the gaps in the available records, marshal contextual knowledge and perspectives of the time and place, and construct a sound historic interpretation."[c]

### Attitude Standards or Objectives

Students will appreciate the variety of information that can be found on maps. Students will understand that maps are useful in everyday life.

[a] *Expectations of Excellence*, p.113
[b] *National Standards for History*, p. 15
[c] *National Standards for World History*, p. 19

## Procedures

### Set

- Hang up maps using various projections, Robinson, Mercator, Molewide, Polar, etc., from various perspectives, or conveying political, topographic, climatic information around the room. (Check below for a list of Web sites for sources of material).
- Give students a few minutes to circulate around the room and inspect the maps.
- As a class, discuss the differences among the maps.
  - What are the purposes of maps?
  - How do maps convey information?
  - What is the role of the mapmaker (cartographer) when he or she wishes to map a particular geographic location?
  - Are there specific things that are common to all the maps (distortion, latitude and longitude, compass rose, etc.)
- Transition to the project assignment.

### Body of Lesson

- Hand out the assignment sheet for the map project.
- Review the requirements for the map project with the class.
- Answer any questions students might have.
- Be sure to include a "due date" on the project assignment sheet. An example follows.

## Closure

After student students have completed this project, discuss the decisions they had to make to design maps:

- Which projection minimized distortion and thus was most appropriate for the civilization they mapped?
- Be sure that they understand that a map is a grid (with latitude and longitude lines forming x and y axes.
  - Thus, any location on the map is the intersection of the x and y graph (coordinate this lesson with the math teacher for a better student understanding and an interdisciplinary approach to the lesson).
- What they learned about map making.
  - For instance, the paper summaries of the process often indicate that the student drew the latitude and longitude lines last. This is incorrect.
  - What problems did they have to solve to successfully complete the assignment?
  - Which sources of information were most useful? Why?

## Timing

The set takes approximately 30 minutes. The closing discussion takes another 30 minutes. The map construction is an assigned homework project.

Teachers may make a decision on how long the students will need to successfully complete the assigned project. Generally, one to four weeks is an appropriate time frame, although most students will complete this in one or two days.

## Materials

- Maps of varying types to hang around the room for the set.
  - Geographic projections
    - USGS: http://mac.usgs.gov/mac/isb/pubs/MapProjections/projections.html
    - National Geographic Society: http://www.nationalgeographic.com/features/2000/exploration/projections/
    - The Great Globe Gallery: http://hum.amu.edu.pl/~zbzw/glob/glob0.htm
    - http://www.terraviva.net/hq/gp.html

- http://www.geog.ucsb.edu/~dylan/mtpe/geosphere/topics/map/geographic.html
- Historical maps and atlases online
- http://globalgenealogy.com/mapsmain.htm
- http://www.lib.utexas.edu/maps/map_sites/hist_sites.html
- http://www.hum.huji.ac.il/dinur/links/maps.htm
- http://lcweb2.loc.gov/ammem/gmdhtml/gmdhome.html
- http://geography.about.com/cs/historicmaps/index.htm?once=true&
- http://www.culturalresources.com/Maps.html
- http://www.davidrumsey.com/
- http://www.uoregon.edu/~atlas/
- http://icg.harvard.edu/~maps/lnhist.htm

♦ Historical atlases or Web sites with historic maps.
♦ Textbook as a reference for possible civilizations or places to map.
♦ Software reference encyclopedias like Encarta, etc.
♦ Evaluation Rubric

# Assignment Sheet: The Ancient World or Medieval World

- Required: *a map* of places/topics covered in chapters in the textbook that includes The Ancient World (Asia, Africa, Middle East, and Europe) and Medieval Times (Europe, Africa, the Americas, and the Middle East).
- Select an area that you are interested in and would like to know more about.
- Map requirements:
  - This is the construction (not duplication) of a map of an area during the historic periods we are covering this semester.
  - When constructing your map, you must take basic tools of mapmaking into account:
    - Compass rose
    - Scale
    - Distortion
    - Latitude and longitude
    - Key (legend)
    - Date of the civilization mapped
      - Ancient is prior to 500 C.E.
      - Medieval is prior to 1350 C.E.
    - Topography of the area
      - Mountains
      - Rivers
      - Lakes
      - Seas
      - Deserts, etc.
    - Cities
    - Trade routes/products
    - Surrounding tribes/civilizations
    - Battle routes
    - Conquered areas, etc.
- You will not be able to find all of these for any one area.
- The purpose of the assignment is to understand the relationship between land (geography) and history (story of people).
- To do this, you must figure out how to include more information than you can find on any one map and combine it in a new way.
- It will generally take at least three different maps to gather what you will need.
- You need a *one-page,* word-processed explanation of how you constructed the map.

- You need a bibliography (list of references consulted) written in correct format (author, last name, first name, title of the book *italicized*, place of publication, publisher, pages used, running lines, alphabetized, second line indent—10 spaces).
  - Check your English grammar book for examples of format.
- Your completed map needs to be **larger than 9" by 17"**, but not larger than one piece of posterboard.
- Grades: this project will be 20 percent of your grade for the report card period.
  - Grades will be based on the ability to follow instructions carefully and on the completeness and originality of your approach to the assignment, *not* on artistic ability.
- Be sure to ask any questions or to consult with me if you are having any difficulty completing this project.
  - It is wise to ask your questions at least one week in advance so that you have enough time to successfully complete this project.

# Evaluation Rubric

- (2) _____ Name of mapped civilization
- (5) _____ Date of mapped civilization
- (6) _____ Within correct time period (ancient or medieval)
- (7) _____ Latitude lines (not numbered -1)
- (2) _____ Longitude lines (not numbered -1)

## Legend/Key

- (5) _____ Scale
- (10) _____ Codes for and correctly displayed on the map (some may be not applicable)
- (1) _____ cities (names correct for date)
- (1) _____ empires
- (1) _____ trade routes/battle routes
- (5) _____ boundaries/expansion
- (6) _____ topography (may not be coded but must be obvious if uncoded)
  - ¤ physical features
  - ¤ elevation
- (5) _____ Compass rose
- (20) _____ Projection (correct choice for the topic, correctly executed; things are in the right place, right size, correctly labeled, all major items are included)
- (10) _____ surroundings/located on planet earth (not an area simply floating free with no surrounding geography)

## Paper (30)

- (5) _____ Word processed, proofread
- (10) _____ Explains process followed to complete the project
- (15) _____ Bibliography
- (5) _____ number of sources
- (5) _____ alphabetized
- (3) _____ format of citation (as required, author, last name, first name, etc)
- (2) _____ running lines, second line indent, double space between entries.
- (10) _____ Neatness of entire project

Total _____

Comments:

# What Would Life Be Like If?

## NCSS Theme
### Time, Continuity, and Change

"Identify and describe selected historic periods and patterns of change within and across cultures, such as the rise of civilizations, the development of transportation systems, the growth and breakdown of the colonial system, and others." [a]

## Objectives
### Subject Area National Standard

Standard 1: The student thinks chronologically: Therefore, the student is able to:
"Distinguish between past, present and future." [b]
"Explain change and continuity over time." [b]

### Skills Standard or Objective

Standard 2: The student comprehends a variety of historic sources: Therefore, the student is able to:
"Read historic narratives imaginatively..." [c]

### Attitude Standard or Objective

"The student is able to appreciate historic perspectives by taking into account the lives of individuals, their values, and outlooks within the historic context." [c]

[a] *Expectations of Excellence*, p113
[b] *National Standards for History*, p. 18
[c] p. 19

## Procedures
### Set

- Ask the students how many of them have seen a movie where the characters are in a different time period (*Gladiator, Shakespeare in Love, Bill and Ted's Excellent Adventure,* etc.).
- What was different about the lives of the people in the movie from their own lives?
- Did they ever wonder why people in the movies behaved in certain ways?
  - For example, in a movie like "*The Patriot,*" why did the British soldiers wear red coats and stand in the open in straight lines, becoming such easy targets?
- Explain that people's lives were significantly different in other time periods.
- Today we want to understand what things were different and what things have been relatively stable, or are the same, as they were in other time periods.

# Time, Continuity, and Change

### *Body of Lesson*

- Select several historic periods relevant to the course you are teaching. This lesson could also be used in geography class by selecting several regions or specific countries of the world to focus on (Africa, Asia, Middle East, etc.).
- Students can work either independently or in cooperative groups (jigsaw style) to answer a series of questions about life during the time periods selected. Questions could include:
  - What would I wear every day?
  - Where would my clothes come from?
  - What would I eat and drink for breakfast, lunch, and dinner?
  - Where would this food come from (store, grow it yourself, etc)?
  - What would I do during the day on weekdays (school, work, hunt, etc)?
  - What would I do during the day on weekends?
  - What would I do in my leisure time?
  - Who would I live with (nuclear family, extended family, etc.)?
  - What kind of shelter would I have?
  - How would the shelter be constructed?
  - What would my biggest problems be?
  - What kind of holidays would I celebrate?
  - What would happen if I became ill?
  - If my country went to war, what kinds of weapons would we use?

## Closure

Options:

- Students might write a paper comparing their daily lives today with similar-age children from one or more time periods or regions.
- Students might work in cooperative groups to prepare a multimedia presentation illustrating life in other time periods or regions.
- Students might write their own "time travel" short story covering their "adventure" with travel to the past or to other areas of the world.

## Timing

Depending on the option chosen and the number of places or time periods chosen, the time will vary. This gives the teacher a good opportunity to differentiate assignments.

## Materials

- Historical atlases.
- Trade books from different historic periods. Check the NCSS Web site for applicable trade books: http://www.socialstudies.org/cgi-bin/htsearch
- History or geography texts.
- With an Internet connection, access to Web sites like American Memory (http://memory.loc.gov) would be useful.

# Evaluation Rubric

The evaluation rubric needs to reflect the research questions chosen by the teacher. The benchmarks are drawn from the completeness and complexity of the student answers looking for an awareness of the comparison and contrast between 'then and now' or 'there and here.' Grades can be assigned using either letters or numbers. Suggested benchmarks:

### A, Superior or Excellent:

- The student answered the questions in complete, grammatically correct sentences.
- The answers to the questions drew a clear picture of life in that time period.
- The answers displayed a keen awareness of differences and similarities between the time (or location) studied and our American life today.
- The student illustrated that societies find different answers to similar problems.

### B, Very Good, or Well Done:

- The student answered the questions in complete sentences with few grammatical or spelling errors.
- The answers to the questions showed an understanding of life in that time period.
- The answers displayed an awareness of the differences and similarities between the time (or location) studied and life today.
- The student was aware that societies find different answers to similar problems.

### C, Satisfactory, Acceptable:

- Answers may not be in complete sentences. There may be grammatical and/or spelling errors.
- The answers showed awareness that daily life was different in that time period (or location).
- The answers showed either the differences or the similarities between life then (or there) and now.
- The answer displayed some awareness that people faced similar problems throughout time.

### D, Unsatisfactory, Needs Improvement:

- Answers were not written in sentences. Spelling and grammar had many errors.
- Student was unaware about the differences in daily life between then and now.
- Student showed neither the differences nor the similarities between then and now.

- The student was unaware that problems people faced are similar across time.

## F, Unacceptable, Redo

- The answers to the questions were not written in sentences.
- There were multiple spelling or grammatical errors in the sentences.
- Answers to questions were irrelevant or incorrect.

# People, Places, and Environments

As we study people, places and environments, the obvious social studies courses to focus on include geography and regional studies. What is the relationship between the land and the people who inhabit it? How do climate, topography, and location affect the lifestyles and cultures of the people in any given region?

This theme opens a window for history students as they focus on ancient times because world history courses tend to begin with "river valley civilizations." Students may study the differences among the newly founded American colonies that can be attributed to geography. What is the impact of geography on history? What is the impact of geography on economics?

Here is an opportunity for the social studies teacher to pair with the science teacher who is covering environmental studies by working together to consider topics like acid rain, pollution, or global warming. Or, consider pairing with a humanities or foreign language teacher as a team to examine both the geography and the culture of the area.

The first lesson in this chapter can be used in any history, geography, or economics class. The PowerPoint slides presented later in the section focus on why things are located where they are. This knowledge provides a meaningful context and an understanding for students as they try to figure out ways to remember the facts about places and events that they are expected to master. The lesson was developed for in-service use with middle and high school teachers who have teaching assignments ranging from geography to world and U.S. history. All the teachers reported that this information would be useful to students in their classes. The PowerPoint slides can be accessed on the Internet, downloaded, and adapted as the teacher wishes. The lesson really focuses on information that is frequently common sense or obvious, yet rarely thought about or explained by teachers. Teaching this lesson early in the school year sets up understandings that can be used for the rest of the term.

The second lesson focuses on geography courses. It was originally designed for ninth graders during basketball season. The lesson can be adapted to include a visit to any location, family vacation, or sport that the teacher or the student wishes. This lesson may be completed individually or in cooperative groups. It could also be used as an "open book" test.

Where students have Internet access, they can visit the Chambers of Commerce and travel Web sites for the locations they select. If no Internet access is available, the students may use encyclopedias, tour books, almanacs, etc., located in the school library/media center. Sometimes, travel agencies will provide old copies of brochures and posters to use to decorate the room while the lesson/unit is in progress. Note that the teacher always has the option to download and duplicate information from relevant Web sites if the teacher, but not the class, has access to the Internet. This technique, bringing the Internet to students who lack access, is credited to D. Mark Meyers of Rowan University.

# Sports Vacation Regional Geography

## NCSS Theme
### People, Places, and Environments

The learner can:
"Use appropriate resources, data sources, and geographic tools such as atlases, databases, grid systems, charts, graphs, and maps to generate, manipulate and interpret information."[a]

"Examine the interaction of human beings and their physical environment, the use of land, building of cities, and ecosystem changes in selected locales and regions."[a]

## Objectives
### Subject Area National Standard

Geography Standard 5, grades 9–12, Places and Regions[b]

### Skills Standard or Objective

The student (grades 9–12) is able to:
"List and explain the changing criteria that can be used to define a region."[c]
"Identify human and physical changes in regions and explain the factors that contribute to those changes."[c]
"Use regions to analyze geographic issues and answer geographic questions."[c]
For world or U.S. history: The student is able to: "Identify and explain the criteria that gave regions their identities in different periods of U.S. and World History."[d]

### Attitude Standards or Objectives

The geographically informed person knows and understands:
Geography, Standard 4: "The physical and human characteristics of places"[e]
Geography Standard 6: "How culture and experience influence people's perceptions of places and regions"[f]

[a] *Expectations of Excellence*, p.118
[b] *Geography for Life*, p. 192
[c] p. 192-3
[d] p. 194
[e] p. 190
[f] p. 195

## Procedures
### Set

The teacher may select a professional sports team or let students choose a team. To prepare the students for the activity, the teacher needs the game schedule for that team's season (the teacher may supply it or have students use the Internet to locate and print out the schedule. Any browser with a search engine will have the link to this informa-

# People, Places, and Environments

tion. Another source of this information is *Sports Illustrated* magazine or Web site: http://sportsillustrated.cnn.com/

- ♦ The class is informed that they have been chosen to travel with the team to all away games for the entire season (or if you wish to shorten the lesson, for a given road trip on the schedule).
- ♦ If the road trip is not varied enough, the teacher can create a road trip including the regions/cities the teacher wishes to cover in this lesson.
- ♦ A bulletin board with an outline map of the U.S. can be used and "pins" or marks can be made to indicate the cities that the team will visit (or the bulletin board can become part of the finished project as created by the class).

## *Body of Lesson*

The students are informed that they are going on this road trip, but only after they have created a vacation itinerary and packed their suitcases with the proper clothing. To do this:

- ♦ They must find out the location of the each city
  - Latitude
  - Longitude
  - Altitude
- ♦ The climate expected for the time of year they will visit
  - In order to pack properly
- ♦ While in each city, the class will visit the major historic sites
  - Locate these sites
  - Explain why they are important to visit
- ♦ Important tourist attractions in the area
  - Natural environments (e.g., parks, lakes, mountains, caverns)
  - Man-made sites (museums, theme parks, etc.)
- ♦ Focus on eating foods that are considered to be area specialties
- ♦ Regional vocabulary where necessary
  - For instance, in some areas there are submarine sandwiches, others have hero sandwiches or grinders
- ♦ Transportation concerns
  - Does the city have mass transit?
  - Will they need a school bus?
  - Can they walk around the city?
  - How will they get to the city in time for the game (air, train, bus, car)?
- ♦ Where is the arena, field, stadium, etc., located?
- ♦ Hotel and safety concerns
  - Where can they stay?
  - Will they be safe?
  - Cost of different hotels

Students may complete this project in several ways.

- Teachers have the option of using cooperative groups by assigning one city to each group.
- Students can work in pairs or individually in this research project.
- The project might be "stretched out" over a period of weeks or done in just one day by assigning each student a different city to research.
- Students might use their geography books supplemented by history books, atlases, old AAA tour books, etc., or, students could search the Internet.
- For younger students, a worksheet with specific questions might be easier.
- For older students, a written report or group presentation is appropriate.

Teachers have options of which factors to include on the "report," but the minimum required must include:

- Location (latitude, longitude) of the city
- Climate
- Major tourist sites in the city and nearby
- An understanding of the regional differences among the sites visited

Advanced students might have more factors to include on itineraries (times, cost, etc.) whereas students with learning problems would have fewer factors.

## *Closure*

Options here include:

- Presentations to the class
- Individual reports
- Creation of a bulletin board with the sites marked and information about each site posted by each group or student assigned to that site

## **Timing**

- This lesson can be as short as one or two days, with the students researching on day one and reporting on day two
- Or, it can be drawn out for a larger project
- It would make a good review project at the end of the unit on regional geography or before an end-of-course exam
- I have used this idea in a modified form as a test question for a "take home" test

## **Materials**

- Schedule for a professional sports team
  - This can be done in world history with something like World Cup Soccer
  - Or, another modification would be for the class to be the Olympics Site Selection Committee and have them look at the cities applying to host either summer or winter Olympics (or both)
- Internet connection for research
- Atlases, old AAA tour books, history textbooks, information from various Chambers of Commerce, etc.
- Outline map of U.S. with states and geographic form included

People, Places, and Environments

# Evaluation Rubric

The scoring rubric provided assumes that either each student is working on a single site or each group is working on a single site. It can be easily modified for additional locations or factors; points allocated would be decided by the importance of the factors, the difficulty of locating the information, the amount of information required, etc.

|  | Excellent | Very good | Satisfactory | Needs Improvement | Total |
|---|---|---|---|---|---|
| Assigned city |  |  |  |  |  |
| * Location |  |  |  |  |  |
| * Climate |  |  |  |  |  |
| * Geographic factors |  |  |  |  |  |
| * Historic sites |  |  |  |  |  |
| * Natural sites |  |  |  |  |  |
| * Other tourist sites |  |  |  |  |  |
| * Regional foods |  |  |  |  |  |
| * Etc. |  |  |  |  |  |

# Example of a Benchmark for This Lesson

## Excellent:

- Location includes: latitude, longitude, altitude, state (continent or country).
- Climate is explained in general and relative to the season the class is visiting.
- Geographic factors include: major landforms that influence the site (for instance "Mile High Stadium" or the old "Three Rivers Stadium").
  - Historic sites: all significant sites are included (battlefields, monuments, landmark architecture, etc.).
  - Natural sites: harbors, rivers, caves, canyons, etc., are fully explained and covered.
  - Tourist sites: major sites found in guidebooks have been included with an explanation of why these sites are important to see.
  - Regional foods: an awareness of the influence of cultural groups and/or regional geography on food specialties of the area (e.g., Creole seafood in New Orleans).
- Student(s) illustrate the topics with pictures of foods, sites, etc. They list clothes they would need to take. They differentiate between daytime and nighttime temperatures for packing, etc. They have time schedules, etc. showing an awareness of what they would need to see in the time allotted and still make the game and the next destination, etc. They might differentiate "must do things" from "if we have time things," etc.

## Very good:

- The topics are covered, but not in depth.
- The explanations/analyses of the impact of the factors might be incomplete.
- Students illustrate some factors, are less concerned with time needed to see things, etc.

## Satisfactory:

- All the topics are present, but not discussed.
- The explanations or analyses are weak or poorly defined.
- Minor errors.
- Students have no illustrations or pictures.
- Little awareness of time, but still "make the game" on time.

## Needs Improvement:

- Factors are missing or incorrect.
- No analysis or explanations as to why the class would visit a site.
- Major sites are missed, etc.

People, Places, and Environments

# Why Are Things Where They Are?

## NCSS Theme
### People, Places, and Environments
The learner can:
"Examine, interpret and analyze physical and cultural patterns and their interactions, such as land use, settlement patterns, cultural transmission of customs and ideas and ecosystems changes." [a]

## Objectives
### Subject Area National Standard
Geography Standard 9: Human Systems:
"The characteristics, distribution, and migration of human populations on the earth's surface." [b]

### Skills Standards or Objectives
World History, Era 2:
Standard 1A: The student is able to "analyze how the natural environments… shaped the early development of civilization." [c]

U.S. History:
Standard 2: The student comprehends a variety of historic sources. Therefore the student is able to:
"Draw upon data in historic maps in order to obtain or clarify information on the geographic setting in which the historic even occurred, its relative and absolute location, the distances and directions involved, the natural and man-made features of the place and critical relationships in the special distributions of those features and the historic events occurring there." [d]

### Attitude Standard or Objective:
The student will be able to appreciate the impact of geography in understanding history and/or economics.

[a] *Expectations of Excellence, p. 118*
[b] *Geography for Life, p. 201*
[c] *National Standards for World History, p. 52*
[d] *National Standards for History, p. 19*

## Procedures
### Set
- Introduce the lesson by handing out a blank Mercator projection map of either the U.S., the state you live in, or any place you wish to study.
- Ask: "Looking at this map, where do you think the cities will be located?"
- Why?

- If possible, access the Internet in the computer lab with the students and have every student come to the first PowerPoint slide
- Otherwise, teachers may access the PowerPoint presentation that contains the complete lesson on Theories of Urban Place Location (why things are located where they are) http://coe.jmu.edu/sternbs/Theories%20of%20Urban%20Place%20Location_files/frame.htm.

Share lesson goals with students:
Goals (slide 2):
- Link the location of a city with the geographic factors present at the site
- Discuss the importance of geography for understanding history and economics
- Use geographic factors to make predictions
- Integrate technology to demonstrate and illustrate your findings

## *Body of Lesson*

Define "urban place location:" why a city (an urban place) is found at a particular site (geographic location).
Teach factors that help explain urban location (slides 4–20).
- Ports: where water meets land in a sheltered location; where a river meets another large body of water.
- Confluence of rivers: where two or more rivers meet; where a man-made source meets a body of water.
- Natural resting places along the water: for travelers to rest, ford river, etc..
- Fall line: juncture where the mountains reach the valley and/or the river becomes navigable.
- Transportation breaks: where goods need to be switched from one form of transportation to another.
- Water power source: for industry, electric generation.
- Transportation hubs.
- Extraction.
- Tourism.
- Education.
- Medical.
- Religious.
- Historical significance: cities that once had strategic or economic importance but now "sell" history as their mainstay.
- Business hub: resulting from tax incentives or other attractions of the site.
- Political capital.
- Military functions.

As you can see from the sample slides, the PowerPoint slides are illustrated with maps and contain examples of cities for each function listed above.

People, Places, and Environments

### *Closure*

- The next slide contains a list of cities. Students, individually or in pairs, in class or for homework, need to explain why these cities are located where they are from the list of factors discussed in class.
- Give students a physical map of a new country (continent) with which they are unfamiliar. Ask them to predict where the cities would be located based on the geographic factors on the map.

This essentially reverses the first activity ensuring that students understand the relationships. This second activity could be used as a test question.

## Timing

This lesson works well in a block schedule because the students have time to learn the information and then to practice using it at the end of the presentation. For 75- to 90-minute blocks, the lesson should take two block periods, depending on the abilities of the students.

## Materials

PowerPoint located at: http://coe.jmu.edu/sternbs/Theories%20of%20Urban%20Place%20Location_files/frame.htm.
A copy of the slides follows the evaluation rubric.

- Atlases
- Blank Mercator projection maps
- Blank physical geography maps
- If in a computer lab, students can use the PowerPoint slides interactively; the last five slides contain Web sites for students to explore that are connected to the topic or that would help them answer the list of cities in the first closure activity.
- Web site Resources
  - http://maps.expedia.com/pub/agent.dll?&zz=960473693500 (Expedia Maps)
  - http://geography.about.com/science/geography/mbody.htm (about.com geography)
  - http://www.northernlight.com/nlquery.fcg?cb=0&qr=city+and+urban+geography (NorthernLight search engine uses folder system)
  - Web site to explore: webquests
  - http://library.thinkquest.org/27384/dam.html (three gorges dam webquest in China)
  - http://inkido.indiana.edu/w310work.Iditarod_webquest/ (Iditarod webquest)
  - http://www.un.org/Pubs/CyberSchoolBus/special/habitat/ideal/ideal.htm (Ideal City unit)
  - http://www.geography-games.com/index.html (geography games)

- http://geography.state.gov/htmls/teacher.html (U.S. government learning site)
- http://www.elof.com/~poster_ed/NGSstds.html (National Geography standards with lesson plans)
- http://www.georesources.co.uk/index.htm (GeoResources (UK))
- http://members.aol.com/bowermanb/101.html (Geography world)
- Web sites about Cities:
- http://school.discovery.com/lessonplans/programs/cities/standards.html (Understanding cities: Discovery Channel)
- http://geography.about.com/science/geography/msub9.htm (Cities and Urban Geography)
- http://www.oranim.macam98.ac.il/geo/wurban.htm (Urban Geography)
- http://www.un.org/Pubs/CyberSchoolBus/special/habitat/indes.html (Cities of Today, Cities of Tomorrow)
- http://www.brixworth.demon.co.uk/leeds/#Leeds (Leeds: a study in urban development)
- http://www.rut.com (Radical Urban Theory (L.A. stuff, etc.))
- http://ww.esri.com (GIS and mapping software)
- http://ask.usgs.gov/education.html (U.S. Geological Services, Dept. of the Interior)
- http://hum.amu.edu.pl/~zbzw/globe/glob1.htm (The Great Globe Gallery)

## Evaluation Rubric

The evaluation rubric for this lesson would include a sliding scale for the number of places students can correctly identify:

$$18 \text{ to } 20 = \text{excellent, (A)}$$
$$15 \text{ to } 17 = \text{very good, (B)}$$
$$12 \text{ to } 14 = \text{satisfactory, (C)}$$
$$< 12 = \text{unsatisfactory, (F)}$$

- Given a list of 20 places, students can correctly identify the reasons why they are located where they are.

A second component includes:

- Given a blank physical map (of Europe, or Asia) with railroads, highways, airports, canals, etc. included, students can correctly identify where cities would be located

As with the list above, teachers would decide how many locations would need to be identified for each letter grade.

*Objectives*
By the end of the class you will be able to:
- link the location of a city with the geographic factors present at the site.
- discuss the importance of geography to understanding history and economics.
- use geographic facts to make predictions.
- integrate technology to demonstrate and illustrate your findings.

*Definition*
- Why are things where they are?
- Urban place location theory can be defined as:
  - Why a city (an urban place) is found at a particular site (geographic location).

*Ports*
- Where water meets the land in a sheltered location.
  - New York City
- Where a river meets another large body of water.
  - Chicago (Illinois river meets Lake Michigan)
  - Richmond, VA (James River meets Atlantic Ocean)

*Water Power Source*
- Originally set up for early industries, the falls in the river powered the mills.
  - Fall River, MA
  - Manchester, NH
- After electricity generation freed factories from water as an immediate power generation source, this became less important and many old mill towns faded into obscurity.

*Political Capitals*
- Often a political capital is either a compromise position between major sites
  - Washington, DC
  - Frankfort, KY
  - Ottawa, Canada
- or is used by the government to increase population in an unsettled area
  - Brasilia, Brazil

Why are they there?
- Philadelphia
- Boston
- Phoenix
- New Orleans
- Seattle
- San Diego
- Raleigh-Durham
- Lancaster, PA
- Santa Fe, NM
- Billings, MT
- Roanoke, VA
- Dallas, TX
- Cheyenne, WY
- Ann Arbor, MI
- Kansas City, KS
- Hot Springs, AK

*Sample slides from the power point presentation*

# Individual Development and Identity

Do individuals make history or do events make individuals? The theme of individual development and identity is normally explored in a history class when studying figures like Napoleon, Hitler, or, nowadays, Osama Bin Laden. Was it the historic times that caused these leaders to emerge, or did these leaders, by their actions, create the conditions that led them to the forefront of our history texts?

How do individuals develop in any given society? How does that development differ among cultures? These questions are usually examined in electives like psychology or sociology. However, they also appear as topics in history classes when we study the role of the individual or when we study the opportunity for individual development in any given society.

As we reach out to other colleagues and subject areas, the most natural pairing for this theme will be with English courses. The English teachers can focus on trade books and stories in literature textbooks that reinforce the role of the individual or the formation of identity in history.

The lessons in this section ask students to think about individuals and their role in society. The first lesson, "Person of the Year," explores the nomination process for the annual nomination from *Time* magazine's annual issue on this topic. Students are asked to select a person of the year, decade, century, or millennium and defend that choice. This can be done in either world history or United States history by defining the available pool of candidates. Selecting the candidate pool enables the teacher either to go back in time or to focus on current events. Civics/government teachers can use the lesson by narrowing the candidate pool to political figures. Although this lesson is Internet based, the students could just as easily find this information in the school library/media center.

The second lesson in this section is focused on the concept of historic empathy. Unlike the first lesson, which targets famous individuals, the second lesson examines the behavior of the average person. The question the student must face is simple: When an historic moment or choice arrives, what behavior does a person choose?

The example in this lesson is from the Holocaust but is adaptable to any event in history where ordinary people were called upon to make choices. Did the individual cooperate with or defy the Dred Scott decision? Did a person simply stand by on the sidelines watching others who marched for Civil Rights for African-Americans or women's suffrage? What is the responsibility of a citizen in a democracy to protect and nurture that democracy? How powerful can one person be? Does it matter what the "ordinary" people choose to do or not do? Hopefully, this lesson will have students consider what they might or might not be willing to risk within the context of the historic time they live in. Certainly, the events of September 11, 2001, and the examples of the heroism of police, firefighters, and ordinary citizens make the discussion of this topic more "real-world connected" than before.

Individual Development and Identity

# Person of the Year

## NCSS Theme
### Individual Development and Identity

"Describe the ways family, gender, ethnicity, nationality, and institutional affiliations contribute to personal identity."[a]

"Relate such factors as physical endowment and capabilities, learning, motivation, personality, perception, and behavior to individual development."[a]

## Objectives
### Subject Area National Standards

Standard 3: "The student engages in historic analysis and interpretation."[b]
Standard 4: "The student conducts historic research."[c]
Standard 5: "Historical issues-analysis and decision-making."[d]

### Skills Standards or Objectives

The student is able to:
Standard 3: "distinguish fact from fiction using documentary sources..."[b]
Standard 4: "obtain historic data from a variety of sources..."[c]
Standard 5: "formulate a position or a course of action..."[d]

### Attitude Standard or Objective

Students will be able to appreciate the criteria or factors that make people important or famous.

[a] *Expectations of Excellence*, p. 121
[b] *National Standards for History*, p. 21
[c] p. 22
[d] p. 23

## Procedures
### Set

- To prepare students for the lesson, stop by the school media center and borrow (or make copies of) several *Time* magazine "Man of the Year" issues or check the magazine's archive Web site for "people that mattered" for a given year at: http://www.time.com/time/poy2000/pwm/index.html (example for year 2000).
- You might download several of the stories about these people for students to read and discuss. Ask students:
  - Why was this person important?
  - What was his/her background?
  - Where is he/she from?
  - What does he/she do?

- What is their contribution to others? Etc.
♦ Draw additional questions from the factors mentioned in the NCSS standards at the top of the page.
♦ A discussion could focus on the question: "Should someone who is considered a 'bad' person or who is notorious be nominated?" For example, should Hitler, Stalin, or Osama Bin Laden be selected for the cover of *Time*? I heard a discussion of this question on the "Today Show," December 22, 2001, in terms of selecting Osama Bin Laden as the 2001 "Person of the Year." People have e-mailed *Time* and threatened to cancel their subscriptions if Bin Laden was chosen. Hitler and Stalin were chosen in the past.

## *Body of Lesson*

♦ Today our task will be for each student to review our history course (to date) and nominate an individual that we have studied or read about as the "history person of the year."
♦ To do this, each of you will select an individual you feel deserves this title and research his or her background by answering the questions posted (on either the board, overhead projector, or a worksheet).
♦ We will go to the media center (or computer lab) to enable you to do this research.
♦ Tomorrow, each student will present his/her nomination to the class explaining why that individual merits the title. You will have five minutes to present your nomination.
♦ We will then have a class discussion to try to reach a consensus about the top five candidates for a ballot.
♦ Then we will vote on our "history person of the year."
♦ You will receive points for the completeness of your research and your presentation to the class.
♦ If your candidate is chosen for the ballot, you will receive five extra credit points.
♦ If your candidate is the winner, you will receive 10 extra credit points.

## *Modification of Assignment*

♦ The teacher selects important historic figures and assigns them to students (because of extra credit component be sure to assign historic figures at random by pulling names out of a hat).
♦ Or, students could work in pairs or cooperative groups to select important individuals.
♦ An alternative activity would be to have the students create a booklet similar to the *Time* books referenced in the *Materials* section of this lesson. This book could be "published" either electronically using Hyperstudio, PowerPoint, or ClarisWorks. Using a desktop publishing program, the book could be printed for the members of the class.

## Evaluation

The evaluation rubric will depend on the activities the teacher chooses. In either case, each student will be responsible for research on an individual historic figure that would include:

Written paper

- Basic biographical information (including gender, ethnicity, educational background, institutional affiliation, etc.—points taken from NCSS standards)
- Contribution of the person to history
- Explanation as to why this person is more important than others studied
- Inclusion of a picture where available
- Bibliographic sources in correct form

The rubric can be set up either as a scoring sheet with points for each category or, more holistically, as a series of benchmarks. The criteria for either points or benchmarks are the same as above. If the teacher decides on oral presentations, the Evaluation Rubric on page 87 will be a guide. If the teacher decides on the activity that requires creating a book, the Evaluation Rubric should be modified in combination with the research component.

## Closure

- Following student presentations, the class reaches consensus and then votes for the most influential historic actor.
- The teacher might want to have the vote the following day, with the students having a homework assignment to review the five top candidates and write a reflective journal entry on their choice for the title. This would modify the assessment points.

# Timing

The lesson should take no less than two days, one for research and one for presentations. If the class is unused to library (or Internet) research, the "set" could be done the day before, and the class could meet in the media center for the library day. The voting could be done on the day after the presentations. If the decision is to create a "book" of famous people, the time needed will increase significantly.

# Materials

- Textbooks
- Class notes from the year to date
- *Time* magazine "Man of the Year" covers and accompanying stories on the final choice and the "people who mattered," (also nominated for the title). http://www.time.com/time/poy2000/pwm/index.html

These books are available to order for library or classroom use:

*Faces of Time:* 75 Years of Time Cover Portraits
Jay Leno (Introduction), Frederick S. Voss

**Format:** Hardcover, 1st ed., 131 pp.
**ISBN:** 0821224980
**Publisher:** Little, Brown & Company
**Pub. Date:** March 1998

*Time 100:* Builders and Titans, Scientists and Thinkers
Time Inc. Editors of Time Magazine (Editor)
**Format:** Hardcover, 176 pp.
**ISBN:** 1883013623
**Publisher:** Time-Life, Inc.
Pub. Date: April 1999
**Edition Description:** 75th Anniversary Edition

*Time 100:* Leaders and Revolutionaries
Kelly Knauer (Editor), Editors of Time Magazine (Editor)
**Format:** Hardcover, 170 pp.
**ISBN:** 1883013496
**Publisher:** Time-Life, Inc.
**Pub. Date:** November 1998

## Evaluation Rubric

| Student's name: _____ | Well done | Satisfactory | Needs attention |
|---|---|---|---|
| Approved outline | | | |
| Writes subject on board | | | |
| Faces class | | | |
| Speaks slowly | | | |
| Identifies sources | | | |
| States time and place of subject | | | |
| Relates subject to class studies | | | |
| Gives report from notes (no reading) | | | |
| Uses visuals or handouts as needed | | | |
| Writes difficult words on board | | | |
| Summarizes | | | |
| Is prepared for questions from class | | | |
| Library/class behavior | | | |

## Why Did You Do That?

### NCSS Theme
#### Individual Development and Identity
"Articulate personal connections to time, place and social/cultural systems."[a]

"Examine the interactions of ethnic, national, or cultural influences in specific situations or events."[a]

### Objectives
#### Subject Area National Standard
World History: Era 8, Standard 4: "Causes and global consequences of WWII."[b]

#### Skills Standard or Objective
"Demonstrate understanding of the global scope and human costs of the war by analyzing how and why the Nazi regime perpetrated a 'war against the Jews' and describing the devastations suffered by Jews and other groups in the Nazi Holocaust [analyze cause and effect relationships]."[b]

#### Attitude Standards or Objectives
Students will be able to empathize with historic actors and their choices.

Students will understand that history is composed of the actions of ordinary people as they go through life.

Students will come to understand the power of a single individual to help change the lives of other.

[a] *Expectations of Excellence, p. 121*
[b] *National Standards for World History, p. 268*

## Procedures

### Set
Place the following quotation on the board:
"Good history offers a window on human character, motivation and principles."
*(Berlin)*

- Introduce the concept of historic empathy to the class (advanced organizer). Empathy will be defined as "understanding the reasons why a person acted in a particular way given the historic context."
- Next, show a film on the Holocaust, select a short reading, or deliver a short lecture that will give students the basic factual background on the Holocaust.
- Following the presentation of the facts of the Holocaust, students are told that people were called upon to make choices during this period of history.
  - Some people were victims.
  - Some people were perpetrators.

# Individual Development and Identity

- Some people were bystanders.
- Some people were rescuers.
  ♦ The goal (objective) of our study is to understand how or why any individual chose the course of action he or she chose.

Note: Teachers might review a PowerPoint about historic empathy, http://coe.jmu.edu/sternbs/Historical%20Empathy_files/frame.htm, to gain insight into the process. A printout of the slides is at the end of the lesson.

## Body of Lesson

In order for the lesson to be successful, teachers must ensure that students:

♦ Understand the difference between the past and the present and know that some outcomes are specific to time and place.
♦ Can distinguish among major perspectives and approach these perspectives from a relatively detached point of view.
♦ Select and explain chosen perspectives and the probable outcomes for the historic participants under study.
♦ Explanations are grounded in historic evidence and factual accuracy.
♦ Must undertake self-examination related to the concept of positionality (personal biases or prejudices).

Once the teacher has covered these basics with the students:

♦ The students will select or be assigned ordinary individuals to research.

  A suggestion is Allison Owings book *Frauen*. This book is a collection of oral histories of women who came of age (were teenagers, young married women, and mothers) during the rise of the Third Reich, World War II, and the Holocaust. The book covers a range of women: rural and urban; educated and less educated; West German and East German; etc. The questions that students need to focus on are:

  - Why did this woman respond as she did to the historic events in her life?
  - What did she learn from her experiences during and after the war?
  - How does she feel today about this chapter of her life?

  This book has 32 chapters, with most chapters relating the story of one woman.

This study might be particularly interesting to students who might have difficulty relating to the military side of the war.

♦ If coordinating with English literature class, the reading could be longer. Students could read different books (*Diary of Anne Frank, Night, Lest Innocent Blood Be Shed, Shindler's List*, etc.) answering similar questions to the ones posed above for the main characters (historic actors) in the books.
♦ The important issue is to use nonfiction books that portray the range of responses listed above (perpetrators, bystanders, victims, and rescuers).
♦ The teacher could also use Web-based research, directing students to the Holocaust Memorial Museum's education Web site: http://www.ushmm.

org/education. This site has an extensive literature and film bibliography and may have some complete oral histories available.

Note: Instead of focusing on the graphic atrocities of the Holocaust, this lesson explores the responsibility of each person in a society to act when called upon, thus opening avenues to discuss the meaning of "Never Again." This also provides an opportunity for the teacher to update the class on issues occurring in today's world, like the Balkans, different governments' responses to the spread of AIDS, etc.

Remember:

- Using oral histories or first-person video accounts that relate the events of the rise of the Third Reich, World War II, and the Holocaust to a single life provides students with the opportunity to study the individual within the big picture.
- By focusing on ordinary people and their responses to these events, students are forced to recognize the power of individuals when confronted with events orchestrated by governments.
- In the search for understanding as to why any given person responded as he/she did, students can focus on their own responsibilities as citizens in a democracy.

## *Closure*

- Students report the answers to the questions to the class.
- The reports should focus on why the individual they studied did the things he or she did (or did not do).
- The class should discuss the consequences for taking action or simply being a bystander (usually grouped with the perpetrators).
- It is important to stress that understanding why something happened, or why an actor made the choice he/she did, *does not* excuse or forgive undesirable behavior. It simply helps us understand the choices available and the decisions made.
- The class should feel free to support or condemn individuals based on their actions as long as it is done with an understanding of the specific time and place in history that these events are taking place.
- The discussion could end with the questions:
  - If called upon to act, given the facts of the time, what do you think you might have done?
  - Why would you have made that choice?

## **Timing**

- The students will need time to read the oral histories and answer the questions.
- If combining with literature class, students might be assigned longer readings.
- The reading may be completed for homework depending on the class.

Therefore, time is dependent on the depth the teacher wants to reach for this study. At the least, the students need one class period to learn the basic facts of the Holocaust, one or

# Individual Development and Identity

two periods to research their historic actor, and one to two class periods for presentation and class discussion.

## Materials

- Oral histories from the Holocaust
  - Suggestion: Owings, A. (1995). *Frauen: German Women Recall the Third Reich.* New Jersey: Rutgers University Press.
- Handouts or questions posted on chalkboard.
- Holocaust Museum Web site: http://www.ushmm.org/
- Film, story, or textbook for information on the facts of the Holocaust.

\* It is important to note that allowing students to simply search the Internet looking for Web sites on controversial topics can be ill-advised. In the case of the Holocaust a simple search might uncover more sites sponsored by Holocaust deniers and neo-Nazi groups than legitimate research sites that are historically accurate. Starting at a legitimate Web site chosen by the teacher is essential.

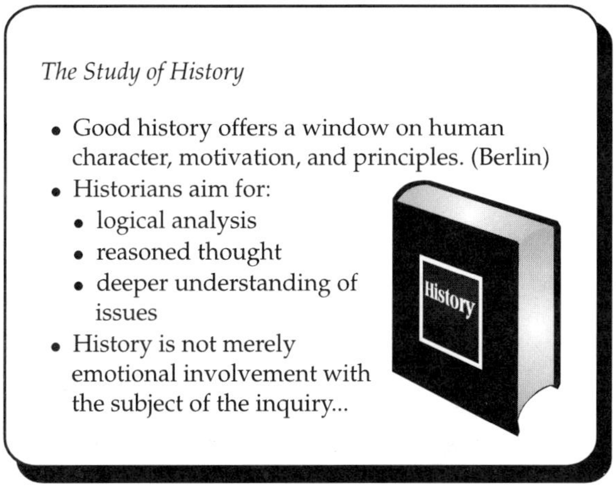

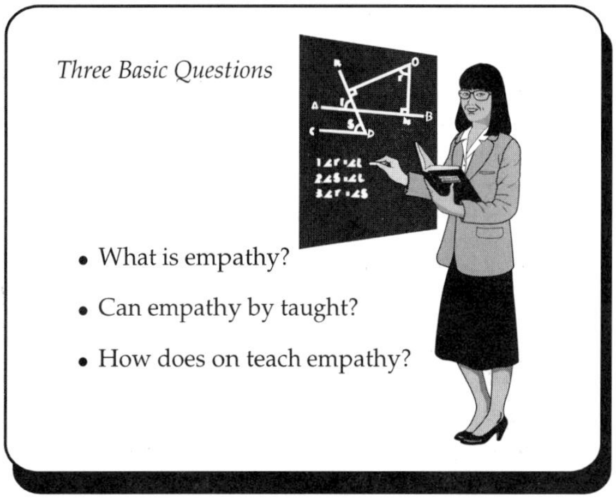

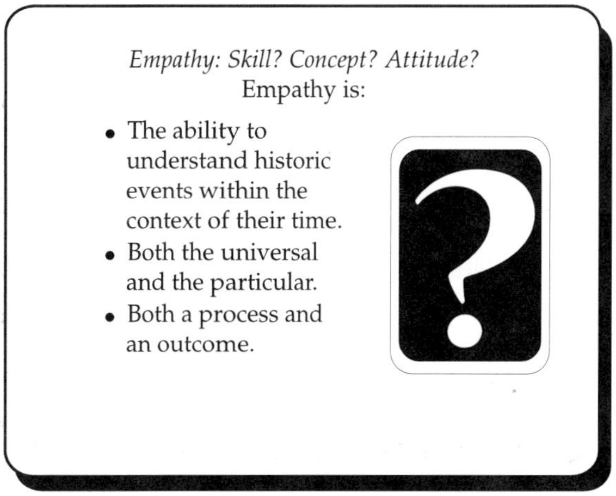

---

*The Study of History*

- Good history offers a window on human character, motivation, and principles. (Berlin)
- Historians aim for:
  - logical analysis
  - reasoned thought
  - deeper understanding of issues
- History is not merely emotional involvement with the subject of the inquiry...

---

*Three Basic Questions*

- What is empathy?
- Can empathy by taught?
- How does on teach empathy?

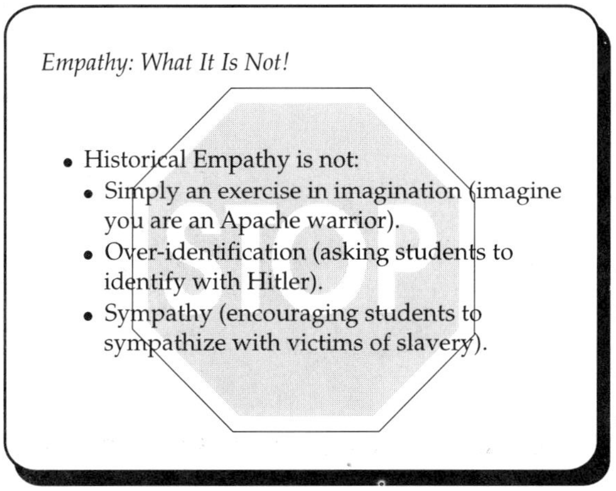

---

*Empathy: What It Is Not!*

- Historical Empathy is not:
  - Simply an exercise in imagination (imagine you are an Apache warrior).
  - Over-identification (asking students to identify with Hitler).
  - Sympathy (encouraging students to sympathize with victims of slavery).

---

*Empathy: Skill? Concept? Attitude?*
Empathy is:

- The ability to understand historic events within the context of their time.
- Both the universal and the particular.
- Both a process and an outcome.

*Five Steps Necessary to
Developing Historical Empathy*

1. The learner's ability to project their own ideas and feelings into the event under study.
2. The importance of paradox: normally accepted understandings do not explain the behavior under study.
3. Availability of appropriate reference and source materials.
4. The presentation of a person or event unique to the situation.
5. The use of two-sided narrative containing misunderstanding conflict, and/or tragedy.

*Historical Perspective Taking*

- Learners understand the difference between the past and the present and they know that some outcomes are specific to time and place.
- Learners can distinguish among major perspectives and approach these perspectives from a relatively detached point of view.
- Learners select and explain chosen perspectives and the probable outcomes for the historic participants under study.
- Learners' explanations must be grounded in historic evidence and factual accuracy.
- Learners must undertake a self-examination related to the concept of positionality.

*Model 1: The Holocaust & Frauen*

- Individual responses to events surrounding the Holocaust cover a range of behaviors.
- Perpetrators—directly involved with design and implementation of the "Final Solution."
- Collaborators—cooperated with the Nazis.
- Bystanders—believed they were uninvolved, either through ignorance or refusal to participate
- Victims—labeled "undermenchen" and targeted for: first, loss of rights; later, death.

*Oral History*

- Using oral histories, in addition to the traditional textbook and video accounts of relating the events of the rise of the Third Reich, World War II, and the Holocaust, provides students with the opportunity to study the individual within the big picture.
- By focusing on ordinary people and their responses to these events, students are forced to recognize the power of individuals when confronted with events orchestrated by governments.
- In searching for understanding as to why any given frau responded as she did, students can be focused on their own responsibilities as citizens in a democracy.

*Model 2: Peruvian Japanese*

- Did you know that at the behest of the U.S. government, 2,264 Latin Americans of Japanese descent were:
  - first deported from their countries of residence
  - then relocated to internment camps in the U.S.
  - finally, at the end of the war, stranded without any legal status?

*The Bottom Line*

- Historical Empathy requires an understanding of how individuals and/or governments acted within the context of their times.
- It does not demand either our sympathy, our acceptance, or our forgiveness for their choices.
- In summary, as we focus on the political, diplomatic, and military aspects of events, we must remember that history happens to real people as they live out their daily lives.

# Evaluation Rubric

For either a presentation or a written paper: Students answered questions asked:
- For example: Using the *Frauen* book:
  - Why did this woman respond as she did to the historic events in her life?
  - What did she learn from her experiences during the war?
  - What did she learn from her experiences after the war?
  - How does she feel today about this chapter of her life?

## A, Superior or Excellent:

- The student answered the questions in complete, grammatically correct sentences.
- Or, the presentation was clear, concise, and delivered with proper public speaking skills. (Refer to chart on oral reports from "Person of the Year" lesson.)
- The answers to the questions paint a clear picture of life in that time period citing facts and examples from the literature.
- The answers displayed a keen awareness of differences and similarities between the time and place of study and today.
- The student illustrated that individuals have different responses to similar problems.
- The student evaluated the choices made by the individual studied.

## B, Very Good, or Well Done:

- The student answered the questions in complete sentences with few grammatical or spelling errors.
- Or, the presentation was less clear, less concise, and delivered with good public speaking skills. (Refer to the evaluation rubric chart on oral reports, p. 87.)
- The answers to the questions showed an understanding of life in that time period using some facts and examples from the documents read.
- The answers displayed an awareness of the differences and similarities between the time and place studied and today.
- The student is aware that individuals have different responses to similar problems.

## C, Satisfactory, Acceptable:

- Answers may not use complete sentences. There may be grammar and/or spelling errors.
- Or, the presentation was unclear at times, longer than necessary to answer the questions, and weak in proper public speaking skills. (Refer to the evaluation rubric chart on oral reports, p. 87.)

- The questions showed awareness that daily life was different in that time period and place.
- The answers showed either the differences or the similarities between life then (or there) and now, but not both.
- The answer displayed some awareness that some problems people face have several choices for response.

## D, Unsatisfactory, Needs Improvement:

- Answers were not written in sentences. Spelling and grammar have many errors.
- The presentation was vague, wandering, lacking in proper public speaking skills. (Refer to the evaluation rubric chart on oral reports, p. 87.)
- Student was unaware of the differences in daily life between then and now.
- Student showed neither the differences nor the similarities between then and now.
- The student was unaware that problems people face may have more than one solution.

## F, Unacceptable, Redo:

- The answers to the questions were not written in sentences.
- There were multiple spelling or grammar errors in the sentences.
- Answers to questions were irrelevant or incorrect.
- There was no understanding that people are faced with choices when problems arise.

# Scored Discussions

*by John Rossi, Virginia Commonwealth University, and
Tom Mix, Murray High School, Charlottesville, VA*

*Purpose:* Scored discussions provide teachers with an additional way to assess your learning. Rather than relying solely on written tests, papers and projects, we can also evaluate your understanding by the quality of your participation in scored discussions. For people who possess strong oral skills, this is an opportunity to shine. For those who would rather write than speak, this is an opportunity to develop new skills.

In addition to providing another tool to evaluate your progress, scored discussions help students learn to analyze and discuss significant issues. The discussion group works together to advance its knowledge and understanding of the topic under discussion. To accomplish this end, each member of the group must show competence in important social, as well as, intellectual skills.

*Procedures:* A group of students will be assigned a topic that they will discuss. These students will prepare for the discussion, just as they would study for a test or do research for a paper. They will read, interview knowledgeable sources, take notes, etc., to be well versed in the topic. The topics and groups will be assigned at least a few days in advance so that the students can be sufficiently prepared. The students must design an agenda (outline) to help facilitate their discussion.

The scored discussions themselves will last between 10 and 20 minutes. The members of the discussion group will sit in a small circle. They should bring their notes, writing utensils, and any books, quotes, facts, figures, etc., that they might wish to share during the discussion.

Class members who are not in the discussion group will be seated an a larger circle outside of the discussion group. They are expected to pay absolute attention to the discussion, take notes if they wish, and not distract the discussion in any way. Sometimes, the observer group may even evaluate the discussion group members

*Scoring:* Discussion group members can earn positive or negative points. Positive points can be earned by:

| Points | Mental Processes |
|--------|------------------|
| 4 | Making inferences or drawing conclusions |
| 4 | Using logic |
| 4 | Synthesizing information |
| 4 | Making analogies |
| 3 | Giving examples |
| 3 | Introducing new ideas |
| 3 | Introducing past learning |
| 2 | Recognizing contradictions |
| 2 | Stating a position |

| Points | Positive Behaviors |
|---|---|
| 4 | Involving others |
| 3 | "I" messages |
| 3 | Affirming other viewpoints |
| 3 | Questioning for clarification |
| 2 | Articulate delivery (speaking clearly, audibly, etc.) |
| 2 | Active listening |

Negative points can be earned by:

| Points | Negative Behaviors |
|---|---|
| -1 | Repeating |
| -1 | Introducing an unrelated topic |
| -2 | Dominating (monopolizing) |
| -2 | Interrupting |
| -4 | Not paying attention |
| -5 | Personal attack |
| -5 | Never speaking |
| -5 | Distracting others |

In the scoring system, we have rewarded more difficult mental and social skills with more points than more elementary skills. This is designed to encourage a very thoughtful and courteous discussion. It is not a debate where you are trying to defeat someone's ideas. You may either agree or disagree with other ideas.

If a student in the discussion group interrupts, politely apologizes, and allows the student he/she interrupted to go ahead, then no negative points will be assigned.

*Members of the observing group may earn negative points for inappropriate behavior, such as distracting others, not paying attention, or interrupting. Because all students will participate in discussion groups, negative points assessed while in the observing group will be applied against points earned when in the discussion group.*

Most scored discussions will last approximately 20 minutes. However, at first, they may be shorter. For 20 minute discussions, a student must earn at least 30 points to receive a C, 35 points for a B, and 40 or more for an A. The number of points will be prorated according to the length of the discussion. For example, a 10-minute discussion will require only half as many points as a 20-minute discussion, to earn the equivalent grade.

*Processing:* Scored discussions will usually be followed by a processing session, where we discuss those ideas and behaviors that helped or hindered the learning process. This also gives students in the observing group a chance to express ideas that they have so courteously kept to themselves.

# Scored Discussion Checklist

*by John Rossi, Virginia Commonwealth University, and
Tom Mix, Murray High School, Charlottesville, VA*

| *Indicators* | *Student Names* | | | |
|---|---|---|---|---|
| **Mental Processes** | Student 1 | Student 2 | Student 3 | Student 4 |
| Inferences/conclusions (4) | | | | |
| Logic use (4) | | | | |
| Synthesize information (4) | | | | |
| Make analogies (4) | | | | |
| Give examples (3) | | | | |
| Introduce new ideas (3) | | | | |
| Introduce past learning (3) | | | | |
| Recognizes contradictions (2) | | | | |
| States a position (2) | | | | |
| **Positive Behaviors** | | | | |
| Involves others (4) | | | | |
| "I" messages (3) | | | | |
| Affirm Others' Viewpoints (3) | | | | |
| Question for clarification (3) | | | | |
| Articulate delivery (2) | | | | |

| Indicators | Student Names | | | |
|---|---|---|---|---|
| **Mental Processes** | Student 1 | Student 2 | Student 3 | Student 4 |
| Active listening (2) | | | | |
| *Negative Behaviors* | | | | |
| Interrupting (−2) | | | | |
| Repeating (−1) | | | | |
| Introducing unrelated topic (−1) | | | | |
| Dominating (−2) | | | | |
| Personal attack (−5) | | | | |
| Distracting others (−5) | | | | |
| Never speaking (−5) | | | | |
| Not paying attention (−4) | | | | |

# Individuals, Groups, and Institutions

As we carry our examination of individuals further, the study of the relationship of individual people within groups and the impact of society's institutions on individual development arises. Traditional social studies courses that are most often mentioned with this theme include government, law studies, and history. In interweaving some of these themes, the teacher might choose to focus on how individuals can change institutions as well as how institutions circumscribe individuals' choices and lifestyles. This theme is one that lends itself well to service learning opportunities.

The first lesson in this section, based in U.S. history, concerns the issue of child labor. The lesson makes use of a Reader's Theater strategy that is designed to be at a low reading level, in this case 6th grade, and high interest because of the topic. Recent news articles and broadcasts have focused on the problem of child labor and child slavery in developing nations. The lesson gives students a chance to view the problem both historicly and as a current events issue.

The second lesson looks at the institutional mix of religion and government. This lesson, designed prior to September 11, 2001, points the teacher to a strategy to help students understand a little about the former Taliban rule in Afghanistan where religion and politics were not separated. The lesson, with world history content standards, focuses on the religion of Islam. This particular topic was originally selected because Islam is a rapidly spreading religion in developing nations of North Africa, the Middle East, and the Indian Ocean/Pacific islands. In other words, this topic was important prior to recent current events involving the United States and terrorism.

As we are now all aware, there has been significant immigration in the U.S. from Islamic nations. There are more Muslims in America than Jews. Thus, in addition to the fact that the study of world religions is part of the world history curriculum, Islam has an increasing number of followers in America. Students need to learn to understand and respect the religious beliefs of their fellow humans. This is especially true at a time when American voters are confronting the use of federal tax monies for faith-based programs. Additionally, intolerance for Middle Easterners as a result of terrorist acts has increased. It is important to teach students to differentiate religion from politics. Even for those students still unconcerned about world affairs, as American citizens they should understand the beliefs of all the religions present in the U.S.

# Child Labor: Yesterday and Today

*by Jaclyn Smith, Virginia Beach Public Schools*

## NCSS Theme
### Individuals, Groups, and Institutions

"Demonstrate an understanding of concepts such as role, status, and social class in describing the interactions of individuals and social groups." [a]

"Identify and describe examples of tensions between belief systems and government policies and laws." [a]

## Objectives
### Subject Area National Standard

U.S. History: Era 6: "The Development of the Industrial United States" [b]
Standard 3A: "The student understands how the "second industrial revolution" changed the nature and conditions of work."

### Skills Standard or Objective

"The student is able to analyze the causes and consequences of the industrial employment of children (Examine historic perspectives)." [b]

### Attitude Standards or Objectives

"The student will understand how working conditions changed and how the workers responded to new industrial conditions (Explain historic continuity and change)." [b]

### Essential Questions

(issues to bear in mind as the lesson develops)

In a country that has prided itself on freedom, equality, and respect for all citizens, how is it that children were, and still are, taken advantage of in the workplace?

Are we, as Americans, affected by these abuses of child labor in our homeland and in foreign countries?

If so, how?

[a] *Expectations of Excellence, p. 91*
[b] *National Standards for History, p. 107*

## Procedures
### Set

(10 minutes): To introduce the lesson and get students thinking:
- Distribute the *Declaration of Dependence* to each student.
- Read as a class.
- Ask students if they can think of a document that sounds like this (Declaration of Independence).

# Individuals, Groups, and Institutions

- Why did the children write this?
- What are their complaints?
- Does this still occur today?
♦ We are going to investigate.

## *Body of Lesson*

Activity (20–25 minutes):

♦ Have students partner up.
♦ Assign a short reading to each pair of students.
  - They will be the experts on their article.
  - They must work together to read.
  - They must fill out a question sheet to be used during class discussion.
♦ When students are ready, hold a class discussion in which you examine the readings and how they relate to the essential questions.

Note: The students are examining the abuses of child workers through multiple sources. Students in the classroom may read a short section on child labor in the social studies text, but this is not enough. I have, therefore, used nonfiction juvenile books as well as articles from the Internet to provide more information for the lesson. We can look at how each author feels about the big issue. Have pairs share the answers on their worksheets with the class.

## *Evaluation*

♦ Evaluate students by having them write a short (one-page) essay to be entered in the UNICEF Kids Speaking For Kids contest.
♦ Essays must include at least three facts about abuse of children in the workplace.
♦ Essays must include a personal statement about the value of human life.

## *Closure*

(10 minutes)

♦ Ask students how they feel about what they have heard and read.
  - Specifically, how does this affect them as consumers?
  - As future employees?
  - Future employers?
  - What could be done to change the current situation?
♦ List ideas on the board.
♦ Have students summarize the lesson.
♦ Further: students will put their thoughts into writing through the homework assignment.

*Explore Interdisciplinary Connections to the Topic*
**Language Arts:**
Reader's Theater will help students to act out and experience the emotions of a child laborer in the early 1900s (see script at page 108). Reader's Theater is a technique to in-

volve students in presenting material by having them read aloud, or "simulate" a discussion, interview, etc., from history. An example of Reader's Theater lessons is a Presidential Cabinet meeting over a crisis. Students "role play" the different Cabinet members by reading the appropriate words from a script supplied by the teacher that simulates a plausible discussion of the crisis.

- Teacher makes multiple copies of the script.
- Students are assigned parts in the Reader's Theater script.
- Students read their parts aloud to the class or read and act them out.
- Students discuss the issues in the script.

## Materials

A text set is appended to the lesson. A description of the materials, with full citations, follows the lesson.

- **Expository**
  - *Kids At Work: Lewis Hine and the Crusade Against Child Labor* by Freedman
  - *Cheap Raw Material* by Meltzer
- **Narrative**
  - *Lyddie* by Patterson
  - *A Chance Child* by Walsh
- **Web Sites**
  - http//www.american.edu/projects/mandela/TED.mike.htm
  - www.sweatshops.org
- **Appended to Lesson**
  - Declaration of Dependence.
  - Text Set (download articles from links listed above).
  - Readers Theater Example.

# Declaration of Dependence by the Children of America in Mines and Factories and Workshops Assembled

WHEREAS We, Children of America, are declared to have been born free and equal, and

WHEREAS, We are yet in bondage in this land of the free; are forced to toil the long day or the long night, with no control over the conditions of labor, as to health or safety or hours or wages, and with no right to the rewards of our service, therefore be it

RESOLVED, I—That childhood is endowed with certain inherent and inalienable rights, among which are freedom from toil for daily bread; the right to play and to dream; the right to the normal sleep of the night season; the right to an education, that we may have equality of opportunity for developing all that there is in us of mind and heart.

RESOLVED, II—That we declare ourselves to be helpless and dependent; that we are and of right ought to be dependent, and that we hereby present the appeal of our helplessness that we may be protected in the enjoyment of the rights of childhood.

RESOLVED, III—That we demand the restoration of our rights by the abolition of child labor in America.

NATIONAL CHILD LABOR COMMITTEE, 1913

# Questions for Students from Text Set Article Read

Scenarios/excerpts about current child labor issues

## Child Labor

**Directions**: After reading your article independently, discuss it with a partner. Together, answer the following questions. Be prepared to tell the class about what you read.

1. Who was the article about?

2. In what country/state did the story take place?

3. What was the child's job?

4. List any unsafe working conditions discussed in the article.

5. What were the child's wages?

6. What did the child's employer have to say when confronted about mistreating his employees?

# Text Set

## *Nonfiction*

Bartoletti, S.C. (1996). *Growing up in coal country*. Boston: Houghton Mifflin Company.

- *Reading Level*: 6th
- *Topic*: This book can be used to teach students about work in the coal mines. More specifically, topics such as hazards in the workplace, mining disasters, cruelty of bosses, and labor unions/strikes are covered.
- *Genre:* Nonfiction
- *Format/Illustrations:* This book is written in an informative style. It is still very descriptive and provides many first-person accounts of working in the mine as a child. Text is large and double-spaced, making reading easy. Vocabulary is not challenging and is appropriate for the middle school student. Vivid black and white photographs of the mines and machinery needed for work are presented in this text. Many pictures show the hurt and pain in the child laborers' faces. Captions that correspond well with the text further explain the photographs.
- *Highlights:* Excellent photography; first-person perspective (written based on interviews with the author's grandparents); table of contents is very descriptive in terms of what each chapter covers (subheadings included); several primary sources included (newspaper article and a political cartoon).
- *Writing Instruction:* This text would be best used in teaching students how to write an informative or research paper. The heavy use of quotes leads to instruction on proper punctuation for quotes and conversations.

Cole. S. (1980). *Working kids on working.* New York: Lothrop, Lee & Shepard Books.

- *Reading Level*: 6th
- *Topic*: This book can be used to teach students about children and what they deal with in workplaces today. Each chapter contains personal testimonies from child workers.
- *Genre*: Nonfiction
- *Format/Illustrations:* This book is written in an entertaining style. It is very descriptive and provides many first-person accounts of working in various businesses throughout the country. Vocabulary is somewhat challenging, but is appropriate for the middle school student. Few photographs are presented in this text.
- *Highlights*: Excellent first-person perspective (written based on interviews with the children); table of contents is very descriptive in terms of what each chapter covers (subheadings included).

Hine, L. (1994). *Kids at work*. New York: Clarion Books.

- *Reading Level*: 6th

- *Topic*: This book would be used to teach students about locations of factories and mines, safety hazards associated with child labor, and legislation that led to the end of child labor.
- *Genre:* Nonfiction photo documentary; biography of Lewis Hine.
- *Format/Illustrations*: The first three chapters are a biography of Lewis Hine. The rest of the book is written in an informative essay-type style. The text still manages to keep a story-like quality even as we read testimonies from child laborers that Hine interviewed. The text has large font, is double-spaced, and is presented on large pages, which aids in readability. Vocabulary is appropriate for grade level. The pictures correlate with the text beautifully and capture the emotions of the children well. Captions beneath the pictures are very explanatory and provide dates and location.
- *Highlights*: Includes engaging black and white photographs of children working in a variety of places. It includes firsthand accounts of children working in the factories (based on interviews conducted by Lewis Hine). Provides the Declaration of Dependence (historic document/primary source). Table of contents, index, and bibliography are most useful for student research.
- *Writing Instruction*: Use this text to teach biographical writing and personal writing.

Meltzer, M. (1994). *Cheap raw labor: How our youngest workers are exploited and abused.* New York: Viking.

- *Reading Level*: 6th
- *Topic:* Meltzer covers issues such as various jobs held by children, unsafe working conditions, unfair hours/wages, and reform efforts. His discussion of child labor covers the entire span of history, from Ancient Rome to the 1990s.
- *Genre:* Nonfiction that includes several poems.
- *Format/Illustrations:* The format is informative text. The writing does not seem to be as descriptive or engaging as the above two books. There is inclusion of poetry and personal testimonials, however, which contribute to engagement. The font is smaller and there is more text per page. The few pictures that are included are black and white, and some are of poor quality.
- *Highlights*: This book covers the entire history of child labor. It provides a springboard for students to examine similarities and differences between then and now. The book contains several poems about child labor. A chapter entitled "What You Need To Know About Teenage Jobs" allows students to see how issues that affected children long ago (hours, wages, job safety, allowing time for schoolwork) affect present day children as well. A useful table of contents, bibliography, and index aid in research.
- *Writing Instruction*: The book was selected because of the included poetry. Use the poems to teach rhyming poetry to students.

## *Historic Fiction*

Paterson, K. (1991). *Lyddie*. New York: Lodestar Books.

- *Reading Level:* 6th
- *Topic:* This book focuses on Lowell, Massachusetts, one of the first factories to open and accept children as workers. Emphasizes the fact that many young women left their homes to work in factories as a means of becoming independent.
- *Genre:* Historic fiction
- *Format/Illustrations:* This is a narrative story written in a third-person perspective. The author has several characters communicate in letter form to move the plot along. The writing style is very engaging. Use of mountain dialect makes the story more interesting. Vocabulary is appropriate for sixth grade. There are no illustrations.
- *Highlights*: I like this book because it paints a very vivid picture of what the mill girls actually experienced each day at work (i.e., bosses, operation of machinery). It also contains many vocabulary words central to the topic of child labor: overseer, looms, petition, reform, etc. Lyddie also confronts many issues that middle schoolers would. They can relate when she must deal with getting over shyness, making friends, lack of "proper" clothes to wear, and sexual/dating matters. She helps the students to connect to the book.
- *Writing Instruction:* This book provides small examples of letter writing. It also contains several poems/limericks that could lead to writing instruction.

Walsh, J.P. (1978). *A chance child*. New York: Farrar Straus Giroux.

- *Reading Level*: 6th
- *Genre:* Historic fiction
- *Format/lIustrations*: This book is told in third-person narrative. Use of dialogue and dialect make the book engaging. However, the dialect will slow down some readers. An example of the tricky text is: "Thowt a' a' must ha' dreamed thee." Many students may get frustrated with this. There are no illustrations.
- *Highlights:* This is the only book in the text set that provides an example of child labor in Britain. It is useful for students to examine what British children experienced compared to what the American children experienced. Also, it provides female as well as male characters. Without the risk of sounding sexist, more girls would probably read Lyddie. This book provides male characters that boys can identify with.
- *Writing Instruction:* This book could be used in teaching storytelling/narrative writing and the writing of conversations.

# Readers Theater Example

## Kids At Work: The Lewis Hine Interviews

*Characters*

| | | |
|---|---|---|
| Lewis Hine | William Zorach | Jim Sullivan |
| Narrator One | Stephen Knight | |
| Narrator Two | Angelica | |

**Narrator One:** It began in eighteenth-century England. The new inventions, new technology, and new processes brought about great changes in social and economic life. The same thing soon happened in other parts of Europe and America. (Meltzer, 28)

**Narrator Two:** Many machines were invented. Factories, mines, and mills needed plenty of cheap labor. Across the United States of America, children who should have been in school or at play had to work for a living. (Freedman, 2)

**Narrator One:** One brave schoolteacher, Lewis Hine, quit his job and traveled across the country for the National Child Labor Committee. He investigated workplaces and interviewed the children there. He took pictures of what he saw because he hoped that Americans everywhere would see what a cruel thing child labor was. (Freedman, 5)

**Lewis Hine:** This is Lewis Hine reporting from Cleveland, Ohio where child labor is very common. With me is thirteen-year-old William Zorach. William, please state your name again and tell us what kind of odd jobs you have held as a child laborer.

**William Zorach:** My name is William Zorach. When I was eight years old, I began selling papers and shining shoes on the streets of Cleveland. Then I got a machine shop job. A boy told me, "Watch yourself. The last kid working that punch machine lost all his fingers on one hand." Now I work in a brass factory. My job is to dip the hot brass in benzine and roll it in sawdust. It is so painful to my hands that I'm in agony. (Meltzer, 57)

**Lewis Hine:** Really? Wow, that must be awful. What do you do to make your hands feel better after work?

**William:** Well, I usually soak my hands in an alum solution at night. It helps to harden my skin and heal any wounds. (Freedman, 43)

**Lewis Hine:** Well, best of luck to you William. Thank you for taking the time to talk with me.

**Narrator One:** From Cleveland, Lewis traveled to the New England region of the United States. Here, in states such as Rhode Island and Massachusetts, many children worked in textile mills.

**Lewis Hine:** Reporting live from the beautiful state of Rhode Island, I'm Lewis Hine. Tonight, we have for you the results of an investigation on wages that the child workers earn in the cotton mills here. Stephen Knight is a worker in a local mill, and he's with me here tonight to bring to the public's attention the injustices of child labor. Stephen, tell us about how many hours you work a day and how much you are paid.

# Individuals, Groups, and Institutions

**Stephen Knight:** Like Mr. Hine said, I'm Stephen Knight from Rhode Island. I work fourteen hours a day in a cotton mill.

**Lewis Hine:** Fourteen hours a day? When you do have time for school or play?

**Stephen Knight:** Well, sir, I don't go to school. There's no time left after work. Besides, I'd be too tired to learn.

**Lewis Hine:** That's too bad, Stephen. A child your age should be getting an education and playing with friends. How much money do they pay you, Stephen, for working these long hours?

**Stephen Knight:** For my services, I am allowed 42 cents a week. This amounts to seven cents per day, or one-half cent per hour! (Meltzer, 36)

**Lewis Hine:** That is outrageous!

**Narrator Two:** Lewis Hine traveled further up the East Coast to New York. This state was the home to many immigrant families from Europe. They came to America seeking a better way of life, but soon discovered the hardships that they would have to face.

**Lewis Hine:** Here in the slums of New York City, I'm Lewis Hine, reporting on immigrant families and the work expected of their children. Angelica is here with me, and she would like to describe a typical night at home with her family.

**Angelica:** Hello. I'm Angelica. I live with my family in a one-bedroom apartment in New York. Every night, we sit at the kitchen table making paper forget-me-nots by the light of the kerosene lamp. I make 540 flowers a day for five cents (Freedman, 16).

**Lewis Hine:** Five cents for each flower you make?

**Angelica:** No sir. Five cents for *all* of the flowers. Mother says, `Flower work is cheap now. Too cheap work for anybody but us.'(Freedman, 16)

**Lewis Hine:** This is just not fair. Children are being exploited. We, the American public, must do something for these children!

**Narrator One:** Hine's last stop was in West Virginia. This state was often referred to as "coal country." The young boys worked in the breaker (where the coal was broken and sorted). The older ones actually went down into the coal mines. (Bartoletti, 13)

**Lewis Hine:** I'm here with Jim Sullivan, a "breaker boy", as they are known in these parts. Jim, could you please describe what it's like in the breaker?

**Jim:** OK. We sit on pine boards and straddle the chutes from which the coal streams down. When the coal starts to fall, it spews black clouds of coal dust, steam, and smoke that turn our faces and clothes black. Our bosses won't let us wear gloves, even in cold weather, because gloves keep our fingers from moving fast enough. The sulfur muck on the coal makes our hands swell, crack, and bleed. We call it "red tips." (Bartoletti, 16)

**Lewis Hine:** And how are your bosses? How do they treat you?

**Jim:** They beat us. If we are caught wearing gloves, the boss strikes our knuckles with a long stick. Some bosses kick us in the ribs or stomp on our fingers with hobnailed boots if they catch us daydreaming or talking. They are not friendly at all. (Barlotti, 17)

**Narrator Two**: Because of people like Lewis Hine, Americans began to protest child labor. Reformers went to Congress and the courts to fight for a national child labor law. Even the children spoke out in their Declaration of Dependence that was written in 1913.

**All**: We, the children of America are declared to have been born free and equal.

**Stephen**: We are yet in slavery in this land of the free! We are forced to work the long day or the long night with no control over the conditions of labor, as to health and safety or hours or wages, and with no right to the rewards of our services. Therefore, be it...

**Angelica**: That childhood is endowed with certain rights, among which are freedom from work for daily bread; the right to play and to dream...

**Jim**: ... the right to normal sleep of the night season; the right to an education, that we may have equality of opportunity for developing our minds and hearts.

**All**: That we demand the restoration of our rights by the abolition of child labor in America! (Freedman, 91)

**Narrator One**: Progress came slowly, and only after a long and bitter struggle. In 1912, the United States Children's Bureau was formed to investigate the factories, mills, and mines where children worked.

**Narrator Two**: Child labor did not begin to disappear until the Great Depression. At that time, it was hard to find work, and adults took the jobs normally held by children. (Freedman, 94)

**Narrator One**: Finally, in 1938, President Franklin Delano Roosevelt signed the Fair Labor Standards Act. This places limits on child labor and set minimum wages and maximum hours for workers everywhere.

**Narrator Two**: Children under sixteen were not allowed to work in the manufacturing and mining industries. They had finally won their battle for freedom!

Individuals, Groups, and Institutions

# Politics and Religion

## NCSS Theme
### *Individuals, Groups, and Institutions*

"Identify and analyze examples of tensions between expressions of individuality and group or institutional efforts to promote social conformity."[a]

"Identify and describe examples of tensions between belief systems and government policies and laws."[b]

## Objectives
### *Subject Area National Standards*

World History: Era 4: "Expanding zones of exchange and encounter 300–1000 C.E."[c]

Standard 2: "Causes and consequences of the rise of Islamic civilization in the 7th–10th centuries."[d]

Standard 2A: "Demonstrate understanding of the emergence of Islam and how Islam spread in southwest Asia, North Africa, and Europe."[d]

### *Skills Standards or Objectives*

"Describing the life of Muhammad, the development of the early Muslim community, and the basic teachings and practices of Islam (assess the importance of the individual)."[d]

"Analyzing how Islam spread in southwest Asia and the Mediterranean region. (analyze the influence of ideas)."[d]

### *Attitude Standards or Objectives*

Students will be able to understand the diversity of ideas about religion that exist in the world.

Students will be able to understand diversity of ideas within a religion.

[a] *Expectations of Excellence, p. 124*
[b] *p. 91*
[c] *National Standards for World History, p. 87*
[d] *p. 108*

## Procedures
### Set

- Show the class a picture of the former Taliban-run government in Afghanistan destroying statues of Buddha because they believe that the statues violate their religious beliefs.
  - Taliban soldier stand carrying rocket in front of the tallest Buddha statue in the central province of Bamiyan before destroying it. (AP) http://

www.buddhismtoday.com/english/world/facts/032-destruction30.htm

- Remind the class that they have already studied Buddhism earlier in the year. Review basic facts about Buddhism if desired.
- Ask: Can anyone tell me why the government of Afghanistan would want to destroy this statue?
- If nobody knows the answer, the class is set up for an inquiry lesson on Islam. If a student does know the answer, the teacher can follow up by asking if all Muslims approved of this destruction.
- Mention to the class that the Taliban decided to require Hindus to wear a badge on their clothing (*N.Y. Times* "Taliban Propose an Identity Label for the 'Protection' of 'Hindus,'" May 23, 2001).
- How would students feel if they had to wear a patch on their clothing designating their religion?
- Do they think this will really "protect" the Hindus? (If necessary, remind students about their earlier study of Hinduism).
- Ask: Do all Muslims live in a "theocracy" (define as: a government ruled by a single, state-sponsored religion)?
- Lead students to the question: What is the legitimate role of religion and/or religious institutions in regard to "state" or government policies?
- In order to answer that question, the class will begin a study of Islam, in world history and today.

## Body of Lesson

- Students will study the story of Muhammad, the principles of Islam and the spread of Islam across the Middle East, North Africa, and Western Europe (the Iberian peninsula).
- Several methods may be used for the gaining the basic information.
  - World history textbooks have this information, and there are several good videotapes and/or CD-ROM programs that include the study of Islam (its founding, beliefs, spread and sects or branches).
  - The teacher could present a mini-lecture with the salient facts. Web sites with pertinent information are listed under *Materials* section of the lesson.
- Once students have obtained the basic information and understanding, they should move to the authentic part of the lesson by examining:
  - How Islam has changed over time.
  - How it is practiced in today's world.
  - Why Islam is one of the world's fastest growing religions.
- The students, in small groups, should be assigned countries primarily from the Middle East, North Africa, and Asia.
- Each group of students should research answers to the following questions:
  - How did Islam become established in this country?

# Individuals, Groups, and Institutions

- What are the Islamic beliefs and/or practices in this country?
    - Include dress code
    - Dietary restrictions
    - Media censorship, etc.
- What are the rights of men in this country?
- Women?
- Children?
- How much influence does the Islamic religion have in the government?

Using cooperative learning, each student (with four students per group) could be assigned questions for research and presentation.

♦ Students present their group reports to the class.
♦ Following these presentations, the class has a discussion:
- Begin with: Would you want to visit these countries?
- Why or why not?
- Would you want to live in this country?
- Why or why not?
♦ Lead the discussion to the role of religion in the government by pointing out laws that exist in several of these countries that curtail rights, for example:
- There is significant censorship of movies, books, and music that are deemed immoral;
- Women are not allowed to be on the street "uncovered;"
- Women are forbidden from driving cars, attending school, working outside the home, etc.
- People are to refrain from alcoholic and caffeinated beverages, etc.
- Be sure to include the fact that some of these nations are more westernized than others and have fewer restrictions.

*Note:* This lesson may be of particular interest to the females in the class as they study the role of women is Islam both historically (where some women owned property, etc.) and today (where women's rights are severely curtailed in some countries).

## *Evaluation*

♦ Students should expect traditional multipl-choice questions on Islam and its spread during medieval and modern times.
♦ Group presentation will be graded with a presentation rubric. The sample below is for two groups and may be expanded as necessary.

## *Closure*

♦ The Muslim population in the U.S. is growing rapidly (now exceeding the number of Jews in America), and is predicted to become the second largest religious group in America after Christianity.
♦ Islam in the U.S. makes a good closure activity for this study.

- The *Materials* section lists Web sites from which the teacher can gain information to create handouts or to which students can go directly in the computer lab. (It is important to distinguish the Black Muslims from Muslims who have immigrated in terms of their belief structures and practices.)
- Students will work in pairs to consider questions for whole class seminar discussion.
  - How do practicing Muslims maintain their religious beliefs while living in our culture?
  - What provisions are made by law to enable Muslims to practice their religion and still participate in American daily life? (For example, Muslim males have to attend religious services at the Mosque on Friday afternoon. Thus, they may be released from school with no penalty).
  - Should teachers not plan tests or new material for Friday afternoon out of respect for the Muslim student's Sabbath?
  - Should the State Board of Education make this a policy (government rule)?
  - Many observant Muslims pray five times per day. As a future employer, would you be willing to release an employee for the time needed to pray during the workday?
  - Should the government require you to do this?
  - What about Muslims who do not wish to observe these restrictions and/or obligations (veiling, dietary restrictions, prayer, etc.). Should they be required to observe them (as in Afghanistan)?
  - Why do you think that Islam is spreading so rapidly in the U.S.? (Answers include immigration, but must take account of the conversion rate among African-Americans, especially those in the prison population).
  - Why do you think Islam is an attractive religion to these converts?
  - Legislation is pending that would increase the role of religious groups in daily life. For example, religious clubs meeting in school buildings at the end of the school day, federal funding for after school programs run by religious groups, etc.
    - How do you feel about these ideas?
    - Should all religious groups be given equal access to school age children?
    - Why or why not?
    - What do you think the role of the government should be in regard to people's religious freedom?

## Timing

- This lesson incorporates very important principles.
- It covers world history concepts on:
  - The religious beliefs and practices of Islam.
  - The spread of Islam.

- The growth of more militant Islam today.
♦ In addition, it awakens students to the presence of Muslims in American society as well as to areas of unrest in the world where American troops have been sent.
♦ My suggestion would be:
  - One traditional class period for the religious beliefs and practices.
  - One period for the rise and spread of Islam in medieval history.
  - In a block schedule this could be covered in one day. A videotape program might cover both topics at once.
♦ Some teachers like to bring in a Muslim guest speaker from the community to address teaching the religion of Islam.
♦ The study of individual countries would require students to have research time either in the school media center or in the computer lab.
♦ This is a particularly good lesson to use to teach students to use the vertical files, periodicals, and other current resources (e.g., State Department Bulletins) rather than encyclopedias, because they will need to know what is happening in the countries today.
♦ Groups should be able to gather all pertinent information in two traditional periods or one block period.
♦ Presentations should not require more than one traditional period.
♦ The preparation for the discussion on Islam in America should take one class period regardless of whether the students do the computer research or the teacher supplies articles downloaded from the Internet and run off as handouts for the class.

The discussion of Islam in the United States should take one traditional class period. This is another opportunity to bring in a guest speaker who is knowledgeable on the topic.

## Materials

**Islam**
♦ http://www.travel-guides.com/appendices/islam.asp
♦ http://www.religioustolerance.org/var_rel.htm#world
♦ http://www.beliefnet.com/index/index_10004.html
♦ http://www.bethany.com/profiles/a_code/islam.html
♦ http://www.fav.net/acIslam_2.html
♦ http://eawc.evansville.edu/essays/hussain.htm
♦ http://www.islam.tc/main.php
♦ http://www.arches.uga.edu/~godlas/islamwest.html (summaries of all countries today)

**Islam in Asia (Pakistan, Philippines, Indonesia)**

- http://www.state.gov/www/global/human_rights/irf/irf_rpt/irf_pakistan.html
- http://www.islamphil.com/
- http://www.arches.uga.edu/~godlas/moros.html

### Saudi Arabia
- http://www.arabiancareers.com/saudi.html
- http://www.alfaadel.com/
- http://www.saudiembassy.org.uk/profile-of-saudia-arabia/islam/saudi-arabia-islams-heartland.htm

### Afghanistan
- http://www.state.gov/www/global/human_rights/irf/irf_rpt/irf_afghanis.html
- http://www.afghanradio.com/special/usreportonafg09091999.htm
- http://asiarecipe.com/afghuman.html

### Egypt
- http://www.biu.ac.il/SOC/besa/meria/journal/1999/issue3/jv3n3a1.html
- http://www.op.org/nigeriaop/kenny/wafr/WAfr23.htm

### Morocco
- http://www.arabicnews.com/ansub/Daily/Day/001207/2000120727.html
- http://french.about.com/homework/french/library/travel/bl-ma-islam2.htm

### United States
- http://usinfo.state.gov/usa/islam/
- http://www.rferl.org/nca/features/1999/05/F.RU.990517135956.html
- http://www.islamfortoday.com/usahaddad.htm
- http://www.usembassyjakarta.org/yusefsalaam.html
- http://www.belmont.edu/Humanities/Philosophy/courses/GMC/IslamicMoralCulture/IIUS.html

### Jordan/Palestinians on West Bank
- http://anthropology.about.com/science/anthropology/library/LoC/blJordan8.htm?rnk=r8&terms=Islam
- http://islamseek.com/Muslim_Countries/Jordan/

### Algeria
- http://www.news.cornell.edu/Chronicle/96/10.10.96/Algeria.html
- http://www.heritage.org/library/categories/forpol/bg1060.html
- http://www.megastories.com/islam/world/algeria.htm

### Iran
- http://www.cyberiran.com/history/shia-islam.shtml

- http://ksgnotes1.harvard.edu/BCSIA/Library.nsf/pubs/shaffer
- http://www.megastories.com/islam/world/iran.htm
- http://www.findarticles.com/m2267/2_67/63787339/p1/article.jhtml

**Iraq**
- http://www.geocities.com/iraqinfo/index.html?page=/iraqinfo/islam/islam.html
- http://memory.loc.gov/frd/cs/iqtoc.html

## Questions to Be Answered
## (As Many Columns As Needed)

|  | Country Assigned | Visit Country and Reason | Live in Country and Reason | Laws Regulating Personal Behavior (Eating, Drinking, Etc.) | Laws Regulating Groups (Women, Minorities, Etc.) |
|---|---|---|---|---|---|
| **Group 1** | | | | | |
| Student name | | | | | |
| Student name | | | | | |
| Student name | | | | | |
| Student name | | | | | |
| **Group 2** | | | | | |
| Student name | | | | | |
| Student name | | | | | |
| Student name | | | | | |
| Student Name | | | | | |

Place point values in the columns for each student's contribution to the presentation:

5 = Very thorough answer with illustrations and specific examples. Able to answer questions posed by classmates and teacher.

4 = Good answer with either illustrations or specific examples. Able to answer questions posed by either classmates or teacher.

3 = Satisfactory answer with weak example or illustration. Unsure how to answer questions posed by the class.

2 = Unsatisfactory answer. Can not explain reasons or give illustrations or examples. Cannot answer questions posted by the class.

♦ Class discussion on Islam in the United States will be graded using a scored discussion rubric. Rubric explanation can be found in the section: "Individual Development and Identity" (page 81).

# Scored Discussion Checklist

*by John Rossi, Virginia Commonwealth University, and Tom Mix, Murray High School, Charlottesville, VA*

| *Indicators* | *Student Names* | | | |
|---|---|---|---|---|
| **Mental Processes** | Student 1 | Student 2 | Student 3 | Student 4 |
| Inferences/conclusions (4) | | | | |
| Logic use (4) | | | | |
| Synthesize information (4) | | | | |
| Make analogies (4) | | | | |
| Give examples (3) | | | | |
| Introduce new ideas (3) | | | | |
| Introduce past learning (3) | | | | |
| Recognizes contradictions (2) | | | | |
| States a position (2) | | | | |
| **Positive Behaviors** | | | | |
| Involves others (4) | | | | |
| "I" messages (3) | | | | |
| Affirm others' viewpoints (3) | | | | |
| Question for clarification (3) | | | | |
| Articulate delivery (2) | | | | |
| Active listening (2) | | | | |
| **Negative Behaviors** | | | | |
| Interrupting (−2) | | | | |

| *Indicators* | *Student Names* | | | |
|---|---|---|---|---|
| **Mental Processes** | **Student 1** | **Student 2** | **Student 3** | **Student 4** |
| Repeating (−1) | | | | |
| Introducing unrelated topic (−1) | | | | |
| Dominating (−2) | | | | |
| Personal attack (−5) | | | | |
| Distracting others (−5) | | | | |
| Never speaking (−5) | | | | |
| Not paying attention (−4) | | | | |

# Power, Authority, and Governance

Who is in charge? How did they get in that position? Do they have the right to be in that position? The theme of power, authority, and governance seeks to help students understand and answer these questions. Power is a topic inherently interesting to most students as they enter their teenage years and early adulthood. Who rules? By what right do they exercise their authority? All these questions require both philosophical and historic answers.

The theme covers social studies areas including history, government, civics, and law studies. In multidisciplinary lessons, the focus could be on "power" and how it is defined. Science, math, and history teachers could each explore what that concept means for their respective academic disciplines. In interdisciplinary lessons, the focus could switch more toward authority and team with English classes or humanities classes to study the philosophical issues related to this theme.

The first lesson, "What Are My Rights," focuses on the curriculum for government and civics. However, it could also be used when U.S. history students reach the section of the course on the Constitution and the Bill of Rights. The lesson would also work in world history when studying the English Bill of Rights or the topic of rights in general.

The second lesson focuses on the technology revolution and the role of the government in controlling access to the Internet. Should governments control access to information? Realistically, in this Age of Information, can governments control information? If so, what types of information should be controlled? Is it the role of the government to protect its citizens from the "media?" One issue that can be explored includes the use of Internet filters in school media centers and public libraries and how this restriction of information restricts students from unlimited surfing of the net.

This lesson is Internet-based. However, in a school without Internet access, the students could explore the same issues using magazine and newspaper articles from the school library or media center.

# What Are My Rights?

## NCSS Theme
### Power, Authority, and Governance

"Examine the rights and responsibilities of the individual in relation to his or her social group, such as family, peer group, and school class." [a]

## Objectives
### Subject Area National Standard

"What are the roles of the citizen in American democracy?" [b]
Standard V. B: "What are the rights of citizens?" [b]
"Personal rights" [b]
"Scope and limits of rights" [c]

### Skills Standards or Objectives

Standard V. B. 1. "Students should be able to evaluate, take, and defend positions about issues involving personal rights." [c]

Standard V. B. 5. "Students should be able to evaluate, take and defend positions on issues regarding the proper scope and limits of rights." [c]

### Attitude Standards or Objectives

Standard V. C: "What are the responsibilities of citizens?" [d]
Standard V. C. 1. "Students should be able to evaluate the importance for self and society of:" [e]
"Accepting responsibility for the consequences of one's actions." [d]
"Considering the rights and interests of others." [d]
"Behaving in a civil manner." [d]

[a] *Expectations of Excellence*, p. 163
[b] *National Standards for Civics and Government*, p. 113
[c] p. 115
[d] p. 116

## Procedures
### Set

- Ask students:
  - Do you know what rights you have as members of this school community?
  - What responsibilities (if any)?
- Have a brief discussion leading students to answer:
  - Where would you find out what your rights and responsibilities as students at _____ (name of school) are?

# Power, Authority, and Governance

- Have copies of school's student handbook and discipline code available as well as student's textbooks containing a copy of the *Bill of Rights*.

## Body of Lesson

- Students can work as a class, in cooperative groups or as individuals examining the school discipline code and the *Bill of Rights*.
- In addition, the teacher might add several legal cases involving school law as it affects student rights:
  - Search and seizure, e.g., *T.L.O. v. New Jersey*
  - Freedom of speech, e.g., *Tinker v. Des Moines*
  - Corporal punishment
  - Dress codes
  - Smoking
  - Suspension
- Or, students can use the Internet to search out legal cases on student's rights.
- As students examine the school discipline code, they might focus on whether the Constitution protects them at school or whether, because of their status as minors and the school's status as being *in loco parentis* (in place of the parents), schools are exempt from laws protecting individual rights.
- Students can discuss whether or not the school discipline code (or county code) is in violation of any Constitutional protections.
  - For example, strip searching is illegal but is allowed by many school discipline codes.
- Are some restrictions on student freedom designed to protect the community over the individual (censorship of student newspapers)?
- Are there limits on individual rights versus responsibilities toward the larger community of the school?
  - This latter question comes up during dress code discussions (wearing clothing considered offensive because of T-shirt statements, etc.).
- Teachers might supplement the lesson with a discussion related to the rights and responsibilities of teachers (faculty handbook as a guide) so that students see that all members of a community have both protections and restrictions on their behavior in school settings (and in the larger world, including the world of work).

## Closure

- Students pick one issue (censorship of school newspaper, dress codes, etc.) and write a position paper explaining the school rules, the Constitutional guarantee under discussion, any legal cases they might locate, etc., and their feelings or their classmates' feelings on the issue.

- Paper should be a minimum of two pages, typed, double-spaced (proofread).
- Alternate ideas might include a debate over any issues that particularly interest the students, or writing an "op-ed" column for the local newspaper discussing students' rights on one issue.

## Timing

This lesson normally takes one traditional class period. If a debate is scheduled, students need one day for research and another day for debate.

## Materials

- Copies of school discipline code
- Student handbook
- Internet connection for legal research
  - http://www.findlaw.com/01topics/37education/
  - http://at-advocacy.phillynews.com/data/inclusionlgl.html
  - http://www.fedworld.gov/cgi-bin/waisgate
  - http://www.supremecourtus.gov/
- Copies of books that focus on the law and education
  - Imber, M., & van Geel, T. (2000). *Education Law.* Mahwah, NJ: Lawrence Earlbuam.
- Copy of the Bill of Rights http://www.nara.gov/exhall/charters/billrights/billmain.html

# Evaluation Rubric

## Position Paper (65 points)

|  | *Excellent* | *Very Good* | *Satisfactory* | *Unsatisfactory* | *Total Points* |
|---|---|---|---|---|---|
| Selected and defended a position (10) | Clear statement of the issue, well defined and position taken. Complexity of the issue is taken into consideration. | An issue is defined and a position is stated. Less complexity in explanation. | There is a position on an issue or there is an issue without a strong position. | Neither the issue nor the position is clearly stated. | |
| Cited Bill of Rights/ Constitution (10) | Cited the specific provision in the Bill of Rights/Constitution. | Bill of Rights or Constitution is related to the issue. | The is reference to the Bill of Rights or Constitution. | No mention of either the Bill of Rights or the Constitution. | |
| Cited school discipline code (10) | Cited the specific provision in the code. Explained its meaning. | School discipline code is mentioned. | School rules may be referred to but the written code is not mentioned. | No mention of school rules, written or unwritten. | |
| Cited case law (10) | Correctly cited and explained relevant cases. Cited precedent where necessary. | Cited some case law. Minor errors in citations. | Case law or precedent not well related to issue. | No mention of case law or precedent. | |
| Writing was clear (10) | Grammatically correct and easy to read. | Minor errors. | Some errors but not major. | Major errors. | |

| Writing was concise (10) | Writing was "to the point" without adding confusing side issues. | Writing may be off the point or confused at times. | Writing hits major issue but strays from the main point. | Writing is confused. | |
|---|---|---|---|---|---|
| Proofread (5) | No errors. | Minor errors. | May have a major error but main point is made. | Major errors. | |
| Total (65) | | | | | |

| | | | | | |
|---|---|---|---|---|---|
| | *Class discussion/participation (35 points)* | | | | |
| | Contributed to class discussion (10) | | | | |
| | Cited facts or referred to documents in discussion (10) | | | | |
| | Listened to classmates and responded appropriately (10) | | | | |
| | Displayed tolerance and respect for different opinions (5) | | | | |
| | Total for Discussion | | | | |
| | | | | **Total Grade** | |
| Comments: | | | | | |

# The Government and the World Wide Web

## NCSS Theme
### Power, Authority, and Governance

"Evaluate the role of technology in communications, transportation, information processing, weapons development, or other areas as it contributes to or helps resolve conflicts." [a]

"Evaluate the extent to which governments achieve their stated ideals and policies at home and abroad." [a]

## Objectives
### Subject Area National Standard

World History: Era 8, 6C: "Demonstrate understanding of how liberal democracy, private enterprise, and human rights movements have reshaped political and social life." [b]

### Skills Standards or Objectives

"Assessing the progress of human and civil rights around the world since the 1948 U.N. Declaration of Human Rights." [b]

"Assessing the success of democratic reform movements in challenging authoritarian governments in Africa, Asia, and Latin America." [b]

### Attitude Standards or Objectives

Students will understand the desire of governments to control access to information.

Students will appreciate the desire of people to access all information available from all sources.

[a] *Expectations of Excellence*, p. 127
[b] *National Standards for World History*, p. 278

## Procedures
### Set

Ask students:
- Should governments prevent their citizens from having access to books, movies, magazines, and newspapers in order to prevent the citizens from exploring political, social, or religious ideas other than those the established government believes are correct?
- Should governments control access to the media to "protect" their citizens?
- Why or why not?
- Should restrictions include visas for travel from foreign nations (where Americans may travel)?

- Should restrictions include passport restrictions to foreign nations (the government restricts who can come in and who can go out of the country)?
- Should there be restrictions on the Internet sites you can visit when they surf the World Wide Web?
- What are some possible restrictions that you think are fair (examples: pornography, violence, hate speech)?
- Who should make and enforce restrictions (governments, parents, schools)?
- Is it possible that opening up the "information highway" to the citizens of any particular nation could damage or cause the downfall of a government?
- How do you think that could that happen?

## *Body of Lesson*

- Students will work in either pairs or groups (no more than five per group).
- The teacher will assign each pair or group a country to research.
- Countries to be researched should range the globe and include:
  - China
  - Russia
  - Peru
  - Iran
  - Iraq
  - Zaire (Congo)
  - Egypt
- The students will answer the following questions:
  - What is the government policy towards censorship of the media (newspapers, movies, books, magazines)?
  - What is the government policy towards access to computers and the Internet?
  - What group(s) is the government trying to restrict access to?
  - Do you think this group(s) is a real threat to the stability of the government?
  - How successful is the government in censoring or preventing access?
  - From your research, do you think the government policies are "right" or fair?
  - Why or why not?

## *Closure*

- Student groups present their findings (answers to the research questions) to the class.
- Students write summary paragraphs relating the policy of government toward censorship to the ability of a government to maintain power and stability.

## Timing

This lesson should take two class periods or one block period.

## Materials

Students can use the Internet sites below, check newspaper archives (particularly the *New York Times* for good international coverage), etc.

Note: Remember to warn students to consider the sources they access and the accuracy of the information provided. Students should check the date of the information, the group publishing the information, facts presented, etc.

General sites to begin research with:

### A Brief Survey of Government Internet Policies
- http://www.ctg.albany.edu/projects/inettb/polsurv.html
- http://www.freedomhouse.org/news/pr041700.html
- http://diplo.diplomacy.edu/Knowledge/diplonews/diplonews-179.htm
- http://www.nua.ie/surveys/index.cgi?f=FS&cat_id=9
- http://www.wired.com/news/politics/0,1283,35952,00.html

### Censorship in General
- http://www.indexoncensorship.org/index.html (Index on Censorship)

### Codes of Practice/Ethics
- http://courses.cs.vt.edu/~cs3604/lib/WorldCodes/WorldCodes.html

### China
- http://ojr.usc.edu/content/story.cfm?request=239
- http://www.soros.org/censorship/eastasia/china.html
- http://www.booksatoz.com/censorship/china.htm
- http://www.miyazaki-mic.ac.jp/faculty/kisbell/esl/socialprobs/jf_def.html
- http://www.igc.org/hric/topics/censor.html
- http://www.wsws.org/articles/2000/nov2000/chin-n10.shtml
- http://www.clearwisdom.ca/eng/2001/Mar/17/NMR031701_2.html

### Russia
- http://www.hartford-hwp.com/archives/63/083.html
- http://www.newsmax.com/archives/articles/2001/3/6/161740.shtml
- http://www.rferl.org/nca/features/2001/01/23012001111644.asp
- http://www.uni-wuerzburg.de/law/rs00000_.html
- http://plato.acadiau.ca/COURSES/POLS/Grieve/3593/Russia/ unfree press.htm
- http://www.jw-russia.org/eng/press/prl01feb12.htm
- http://www.house.gov/csce/011599.htm

### Peru
- http://www.wola.org/perudeconstructingdemo.html

- http://www.infoplease.com/ipa/A0107883.html
- http://www.state.gov/g/drl/rls/hrrpt/2000/wha/index.cfm?docid =827
- http://www.oneworld.org/news/southam/peru.html
- http://www.jsbernstein.f2s.com/initeb/dataflows.html
- http://www.csrp.org/rw/rw867.htm
- http://www.nationbynation.com/Peru/Human.html

**Iran**
- http://www.washingtonpost.com/wp-dyn/articles/A16095-2001Jul3.html
- http://www.state.gov/www/global/human_rights/1998_hrp_report/iran.html
- http://www.iranian.com/WebGuide/InternetIran/InternetIran.html
- http://www.zeitgeistfilm.com/current/closeup/closeuphistory.html
- http://www.rferl.org/nca/features/1999/03/F.RU.990325143632.html
- http://www.freemedia.at/bitter.htm
- http://www.brown.edu/Departments/Watson_Institute/news/visitors04.99.html
- http://www.iran-e-azad.org/english/boi/07821113_97.html

**Iraq**
- http://www.fair.org/international/iraq.html
- http://www.wired.com/news/y2k/0,1360,33323,00.html
- http://www.hrw.org/advocacy/Internet/mena/index.htm
- http://academic.mbc.edu/gbowen/iraq.htm
- http://ojr.usc.edu/content/story.cfm?request=283

**Zaire (Congo)**
- http://www.cpj.org/attacks96/countries/africa/zairerhs.html
- http://www.indexoncensorship.org/698/pett.html
- http://www.pangaea.org/street_children/world/unconv3.htm
- http://www.mg.co.za/mg/news/97jul1/9jul-zaire.html
- http://www.greatwest.ca/see/Issues/1998/0618/art.html

**Egypt**
- http://www.observer.co.uk/freepress/story/0,8224,480025,00.html
- http://www.state.gov/www/global/human_rights/1998_hrp_report/egypt.html
- http://www.derechos.org/human-rights/mena/egypt.html
- http://www.washington-report.org/backissues/0497/9704088.htm
- http://www.washington-report.org/backissues/0194/9401049.htm
- http://www.cnn.com/2000/WORLD/meast/12/12/egypt.censorship. ap/
- http://www.faife.dk/report/egypt.htm

# Evaluation Rubric

Benchmarks include:

## A, Excellent, Outstanding

- The group provided answers to all questions asked:
  - What is the government policy towards censorship of the media (newspapers, movies, books, magazines)?
  - What is the government policy towards access to computers and the Internet?
  - What group(s) is the government trying to restrict access to?
  - Do you think this group(s) is a real threat to the stability of the government?
  - How successful is the government in censoring or preventing access?
  - From your research, do you think the government policies are "right" or fair?
  - Why or why not?
- The presentation was clear, concise, and complete, with a large amount of factual evidence to back up statements.
- All students in the group participated in both the research and the presentation.
- Students have an in-depth understanding of the issue of censorship.

## B, Very Good, Very Acceptable

- The group provided answers to most questions asked (see list above).
- The presentation was clear, and generally complete, with factual evidence to back up statements.
- All students in the group participated in either the research or the presentation.
- Students have an understanding of the issue of censorship.

## C, Acceptable, Satisfactory

- The group provided answers to many questions asked (see list above).
- The presentation was generally complete, with some factual evidence to back up statements.
- Most students in the group participated in either the research or the presentation.
- Students have some understanding of the issue of censorship.

## D, Needs Improvement, Unsatisfactory

- The group provided answers to few questions asked (see list above).
- The presentation was incomplete with no evidence to back up statements.
- Not all students in the group participated in either the research or the presentation.
  - Work was completed by only one or two people in the group.
- Students have little understanding of the issue of censorship.

# Production, Distribution, and Consumption

We live in a world of finite resources that contains a population that seemingly has infinite wants and needs. The economic theme of production, distribution, and consumption includes moral and value issues that underlie how any society deals with these issues. Within the social studies, in addition to economics, lessons may also be focused on comparative political systems or how societies have historically solved the problems of needs, wants, and resources.

Interdisciplinary lessons can include working on graphing with the math department or focusing with science classes on biogenetic engineering to increase resources. In addition, students can be led to consideration of the moral issues concerning what is "just" or "fair" in relation to economic concerns by working with English classes on literary themes that focus on these issues, e.g., Dickens, Hugo. The two lessons included in this section are based in the economics standards, and, in addition, are keyed to either the U.S. or the world history standards.

The first lesson targets an issue that has been widely covered in the media: imported clothing made in foreign "sweatshops." This lesson, "But, I Love My Nikes," uses the instructional strategy of WebQuest to guide the students through the inquiry or discovery process. WebQuest, patented by Bernie Dodge of San Diego State University, is an Internet-based inquiry strategy. WebQuest is an excellent tool that can be used in two ways. First, the teacher can access a prepublished WebQuest that is available on the WebQuest Web site or can create his/her own WebQuest. Second, the teacher can use the guidelines on that Web site to assist students in creating their own WebQuests, which can be saved and used in subsequent years.

The second lesson, "My Paycheck Shrunk," addresses the issues of taxation and the role of the government in regulating, or not regulating, the marketplace. Students who have part-time jobs may have noticed the amount of money deducted from their salaries for different federal and state programs. This lesson focuses the students on the purpose of taxation. Hopefully, students will complete the lesson and have a better understanding of the role of citizens in supporting the programs that they believe the government should offer. This should help students be citizens who will be better informed voters who know which taxes they believe are fair and will support come election day.

# But, I Love My Nikes

## NCSS Theme
### Production, Distribution, and Consumption

"Analyze the role that supply, demand, prices, incentives, and profits play in determining what is produced and distributed in a competitive market system."[a]

"Apply economic concepts and reasoning when evaluating historic and contemporary social developments."[a]

"Distinguish between the domestic and global economic systems, and explain how the two interact."[a]

## Objectives
### Subject Area National Standards

Economics:

Content Standard 13: "Income for most people is determined by the market value of the productive resources they sell. What workers earn depends, primarily, on the value of what they produce and how productive they are."[b]

Content Standard 6: "When individuals, regions, and nations specialize in what they can produce at the lowest cost and then trade with others, both production and consumption increase."[c]

### Skills Standards or Objectives

World History: Era 8, Standard 6: "Promises and paradoxes of the second half of the 20th century."[d]

Standard 6B: "Demonstrate understanding of how increasing economic interdependence has transformed society."[e]

### Attitude Standard or Objective

Students will be able to appreciate that there are social factors that affect the workings of our global economy.

[a] *Expectations of Excellence, p. 130*
[b] *National Content Standards for Economics, p. 24*
[c] *p. 11*
[d] *National Standards for World History, p. 276*
[e] *p.276*

Note: The purpose of this lesson is to have students understand both the working of our global economy and the fact that there are social factors (producers and consumers who are real people) in the abstract concepts of supply and demand, market economy, multinational corporations, etc.

## Procedures
### Set

- For homework, have students read the labels of their clothes as they get dressed to come to school.
- Have them list the item of clothing and where it was made (or, have them take off their shoes in class and look at where they were made).
- Discuss the fact that most of our clothing and footwear is manufactured in other countries.
- Ask students:
  - Have you ever thought about the people who make the clothing you buy?
  - What do you think their lives are like?
  - Where do they live?
  - How much do they get paid, etc.?

### Body of Lesson

- Teachers can either have students do the Internet research in the computer lab or the classroom, or teachers can access the Internet sites and download information for use in class.
- Divide students into cooperative groups or, if doing computer research, into dyads.
- This lesson can be set up as a WebQuest (http://edWeb.sdsu.edu/Webquest/materials.htm) designed either by the teacher, or, more effectively, by the students.
  - The rules for WebQuests and the rubrics for grading them are easily obtained from the Bernie Dodge's WebQuest site.
  - The site also contains rubrics for evaluating a newly created WebQuest.
- If the teacher designs the WebQuest, the lesson consists of bringing the students to the computer lab and having them complete the inquiry-based lesson by researching sites that would require them to define basic economic terms chosen by the teacher.
  - The assessment instrument would be the completed question sheet that accompanied the teacher-designed WebQuest.
- For student-created WebQuests, the lesson would require students to do the research and design a WebQuest based on answering the question:
  - Should consumers avoid the purchase of Nike clothing or footwear?
  - There are other corporations that could also be used for this lesson and the class could be divided with different pairs of students researching different corporations.
- Instructions for designing WebQuests:
  - http://edWeb.sdsu.edu/Webquest/roadmap/index.htm (PowerPoint)

- http://www.iste.org/L&L/archive/vol28/no8/featuredarticle/dodge/index.html (5 Rules for Writing Great WebQuests)
- http://edWeb.sdsu.edu/people/bdodge/Webquest/buildingblocks.html (Building Blocks of Creating a WebQuest)

## *Closure*

♦ Students completing the teacher-made WebQuest would discuss the issues:
  - Should consumers avoid the purchase of Nike clothing or footwear?
  - Students should also write a journal entry or position paper.
♦ Students creating WebQuests would present them to the class.
  - The class, along with the teacher, evaluates the WebQuest by downloading and printing out the Webquest. http://edWeb.sdsu.edu/Webquest/Webquestrubric.html (Rubric for evaluation)

## Timing

♦ A teacher-made WebQuest should take students approximately one class period to complete, depending on the number of questions the teacher includes in the WebQuest.
♦ Student-made products will take one to two class periods to design, depending on student familiarity with the process (the first time will take the longest).
  - I suggest that the first time students create WebQuests, the teacher should review the PowerPoint presentation on WebQuest design (http://edWeb.sdsu.edu/Webquest/roadmap/index.htm) with the class.
♦ Then, time must be allotted for the students to present their products to the class.
♦ If the class has a Web site (or the teacher has a Web site) the students could upload their products onto this Web site for students in other classes to use or for the teacher to use the following year.

## Materials

♦ Textbook for economics or sections of history texts that deal with economic factors: supply and demand; markets; multinational corporations; etc.
♦ A sampling of Web sites on the issue of working conditions in Nike factories. Note that the first four sites are Nike's links to enable the gathering of research for a balanced discussion or debate. (I typed "Nike sweatshop controversy" into the search engine, in this case www.google.com).
  - http://www.nikebiz.com/labor/pr_comp.shtml (Nike on their beliefs about factory conditions)
  - http://www.nikebiz.com/labor/code.shtml (Nike's labor code)
  - http://www.nikebiz.com/labor/pr_comp.shtml (monitoring Nike factories)

- http://www.nikebiz.com/labor/faq.shtml#Biz37 (Nike pays wages)

◆ **Sweatshop controversy** raises questions at USC

**Sweatshop controversy** raises questions at USC….the Kukdong factory an alleged **sweatshop** that has previously…Kukdong manufactures products by **Nike**, a USC licensee…

www.usc.edu/student-affairs/dt/V142/N29/02-sweatshop.29c.html (8k)

◆ Nike Rhetoric versus **Sweatshop** Reality

…world (116 in the US). The **controversy** is getting heated as we…When confronted with undeniable **sweatshop** conditions in **Nike** factories, the response is to…

cbae.nmsu.edu/~dboje/conferences/nike%20rhetoric%20and%20 sweatshops.html (101k)

◆ **Nike** Campaign: MIT Graduate Student Jonah Peretti and Vada…

Graduate Student Jonah Peretti and Vada Manager, Director of Global Issues Management at **Nike**, Discuss **Sweatshop Controversy** and Personalization of **Nike** Shoes…

www.globalexchange.org/economy/corporations/nike/today022801.html (16k)

◆ **Nike** Update

…and Vada Manager, Director of Global Issues Management at **Nike**, Discuss **Sweatshop Controversy** and Personalization of **Nike** Shoes—There's a new gimmick on the…

www.globalexchange.org/economy/corporations/nike/update.html (27k)
Cached—Similar pages
[More results from www.globalexchange.org]

◆ Urban Legends Reference Pages: Business (Just Don't Do It!)

…Couric, Katie. "…Discuss **Sweatshop Controversy** and Personalization of **Nike** Shoes." Today Show. 28 February 2001….

www.snopes2.com/business/consumer/nike.htm (15k) Tulane Hullabaloo Online—News

◆ …**Sweatshop controversy** grows Josephine Salm and Allison Smith, news content editor

and…**Nike** to terminate contract with Brown U. over licensing code….

◆ [IMC-Seattle] MG: SOLE: **Sweatshop** shoe requestor vs **Nike** on…

…Peretti and Vada Manager, Director of Global Issues Management at **Nike**, Discuss **Sweatshop Controversy** and Personalization of **Nike** Shoes Katie Couric, co-host…

lists.indymedia.org/mailman/public/imc-seattle/2001-March/ 003135. html (15k)

- Weekly Planet | This Week in News

    ...The **Nike sweatshop** custom shoes **controversy** was reported in a typically shallow and unlibertarian manner. No one dealt with the obvious question: If **Nike** stops...

    www.weeklyplanet.com/2001-03-29/news_feature3.html (24k)

- As You Sow Foundation

    ...9 percent, but also on negative publicity from the **sweatshop controversy**." After years of denials, **Nike** executives admitted that the protests generated by...

    www.asyousow.org/nike7.htm (10k)

- Just Do It! Boycott **Nike**!

    ...The result was a **controversy** about the school boards ... of the list of non-**sweatshop** companies, we will let...order): Disney, Wal-Mart, **Nike**, Guess?, Victoria Secret...

    www.geocities.com/Athens/Acropolis/5232/ (54k)

# Evaluation Rubric
## A Draft Rubric for Evaluating WebQuests

The WebQuest format can be applied to a variety of teaching situations. If teachers take advantage of all the possibilities inherent in the format, students will have a rich and powerful experience. This rubric will help teachers pinpoint the ways in which their WebQuest isn't doing everything it could do. If a page seems to fall between categories, feel free to score it with in-between points.

| | *Beginning* | *Developing* | *Accomplished* | Score |
|---|---|---|---|---|
| **Overall Aesthetics** (This refers to the WebQuest page itself, not the external resources linked to it.) | | | | |
| *Overall visual appeal* | 0 points<br>Background is gray. There are few or no graphic elements. No variation in layout or typography.<br>OR<br>Color is garish and/or typographic variations are overused and legibility suffers. | 1 point<br>There are a few graphic elements. There is some variation in type size, color, and layout. | 2 points<br>Appealing graphic elements are included appropriately. Differences in type size and/or color are used well. | |
| Introduction | | | | |
| *Motivational effectiveness of Introduction* | 0 points<br>Introduction is purely factual, with no appeal to relevance or social importance. | 1 point<br>Introduction relates somewhat to the learner's interests and/or describes a compelling question or problem. | 2 points<br>The Introduction draws the reader into the lesson by relating to the learner's interests or goals and/or engagingly describing a compelling question or problem. | |
| *Cognitive effectiveness of the Introduction* | 0 points<br>Introduction doesn't prepare the reader for what is to come, or build on what the learner already knows. | 1 point<br>Introduction makes some reference to learner's prior knowledge and previews to some extent what the lesson is about. | 2 points<br>The Introduction builds on learner's prior knowledge by explicitly mentioning important concepts or principles, and effectively prepares the learner for the lesson by foreshadowing new concepts and principles. | |

## Production, Distribution, and Consumption

| Task (The task is the end result of student efforts...not the steps involved in getting there.) | | | | |
|---|---|---|---|---|
| *Cognitive level of the task* | 0 points<br>Task requires simply comprehending Web pages and answering questions. | 3 points<br>Task requires analysis of information and/or putting together information from several sources. | 6 points<br>Task requires synthesis of multiple sources of information, and/or taking a position, and/or going beyond the data given and making a generalization or creative product. | |
| *Technical sophistication of task* | 0 points<br>Task requires simple verbal or written response. | 1 point<br>Task requires use of word processing or simple presentation software. | 2 points<br>Task requires use of multimedia software, video, or conferencing. | |
| **Process**<br>(The process is the step-by-step description of how students will accomplish the task.) | | | | |
| *Clarity of process* | 0 points<br>Process is not clearly stated. Students would not know exactly what they were supposed to do just from reading this. | 1 point<br>Some directions are given, but there is missing information. Students might be confused. | 2 points<br>Every step is clearly stated. Most students would know exactly where they were in the process and what to do next. | |
| *Richness of process* | 0 points<br>Few steps, no separate roles assigned. | 3 points<br>Some separate tasks or roles assigned. More complex activities required. | 6 points<br>Lots of variety in the activities performed. Different roles and perspectives are taken. | |
| **Resources**<br>(Note: you should evaluate all resources linked to the page, even if they are in sections other than the Resources block. Also note that books, videos, and other offline resources can, and should, be used where appropriate.) | | | | |
| *Quantity of resources* | 0 points<br>Few online resources used. | 1 point<br>Moderate number of resources used. | 2 points<br>Many resources provided, including off-line resources. | |
| *Quality of resources* | 0 points<br>Links are mundane. They lead to information that could be found in a classroom encyclopedia. | 2 points<br>Some links carry information not ordinarily found in a classroom. | 4 points<br>Links make excellent use of the Web's timeliness and colorfulness. | |

| Evaluation | | | | |
|---|---|---|---|---|
| *Clarity of evaluation criteria* | 0 points Students have no idea on how they'll be judged. | 1 point Criteria for success are at least partially described. | 2 points Criteria for gradations of success are clearly stated, perhaps in the form of a rubric for self-, peer-, or teacher use. | |
| **Total Score** | | | | |

*This is Version 1.01. Last updated January 18, 1998 by Bernie Dodge.*

Production, Distribution, and Consumption

# My Paycheck Shrunk!

## NCSS Theme
### Production, Distribution, and Consumption

"Consider the costs and benefits of allocating goods and services through private and public sectors."[a]

"Apply economic concepts and reasoning when evaluating historic and contemporary social developments and issues."[a]

## Objectives
### Subject Area National Standard

Economics:
Content Standard 16: "There is an economic role for government to play in a market economy whenever the benefits of a government policy outweigh its costs. Governments often provide for national defense, address environmental concerns, define and protect property rights, and attempt to make markets more competitive. Most government policies also redistribute income."[b]

### Skills Standards or Objectives

Economics: "Students will be able to use this knowledge to identify and evaluate the benefits and costs of alternative public policies, and assess who enjoys the benefits and who bears the costs."[b]

U.S. History: Era 3, Standard 3D. "Compare and contrast the opposing views of the two parites on the main economic [and foreign policy] issues of the 1790s [compare and contrast differing sets of ideas]."[c]

Era 7, Standard 3B: "The student understands how a modern capitalist economy emerged in the 1920s."[d]

Era 10: Standard 2A: "The student understands economic patterns since 1968."[e]

World History: Era 7, Standard 4B: "The student understands the impact of new social movements and ideologies on 19th century Europe capitalism, socialism and communism [analyze cause and effect relationships]."[f]

### Attitude Standard or Objective

Students will appreciate the purposes of taxation for maintaining the functions of government.

[a] *Expectations of Excellence, p. 130*
[b] *National Standards in Economics, p. 30*
[c] *National Standards for History, p. 90*
[d] *p. 114*
[e] *p. 129*
[f] *p. 192*

## Procedures

### Set

- Ask students who hold jobs to bring in a pay stub or find an "anonymous" pay stub to use as an example by making a transparency for the overhead projector.
- Ask students to figure out how much money has been deducted from the pay stub.
- Does anyone know why this money was withheld?
  - Social Security
  - Medical
  - FICA
  - Income tax
    - National
    - State
    - Local in some locales
- What percentage of the paycheck has been withheld?
- Is this fair?
- Right or wrong?

Discuss briefly.

- Say: Today's class will help you understand the purpose of taxation, the basic types of taxation, and the variety of taxes used in the U.S. (or world) to raise money.
- After a brief lecture during which you will take notes, we will convene a "mini-Congress."
  - To discuss a tax revenue bill.
  - Students will have assigned roles for the districts they represent.
  - The goal will be to design a tax system that is fair for the inhabitants of the nation.

### Body of Lesson

- Begin with a mini-lecture/discussion on taxation.
- There are Web sites in the *Materials* section that will provide factual information on the function, history, and types of taxation.
- There are also sources of comparative data from other nations.

Start with the section of the Constitution that permits the government to levy taxes.

- Break down the two basic concepts of taxation:
  - Progressive taxes
  - Regressive taxes
- The class should understand that multiple income tax brackets are progressive and that a flat tax is regressive.
- Ask students to think about which is more fair and to whom.

- In other words, under each system, who profits and who loses the most?
♦ Using the Web sites listed below, outline some of the most common taxes used by federal, state, and local government:
  - Income tax
  - Property tax
  - Sales tax
  - Luxury tax, etc.
♦ Decide how specific you wish to become while being sure that students understand the difference between:
  - Raising money to pay for government goods and services (national defense, education, etc.)
  - The desire of some world governments to redistribute income
♦ Have students discuss what they believe are the necessities that government should provide using a wide range of goods and services. This might include:
  - National defense
  - Police
  - Education (preschool through college)
  - Medicare/Medicaid/national health insurance
  - Social Security (retirement)
  - Welfare
  - Unemployment insurance
  - Fire protection
  - Flood insurance
  - Disaster relief
  - Foreign aid
  - Medical research
  - National parks, etc.
♦ The idea is to have students grapple with what they perceive as necessities and as luxuries.
  - What are they willing to pay for out of their paychecks throughout their working lives?
  - What are their economic responsibilities to other citizens and/or the rest of the world?
  - What should be taxed?
  - What should be volunteered?
♦ Assign each student a state(s) to represent.
  - Because there will be fewer students than states, select a range across the nation.
  - For instance, states with a large influx of immigrants (CA, NY, TX, FL), states that are impoverished (WV), and states that are generally wealthier (CT, VA, ND).

- Students should be given some research time in the media center (or the computer lab using the Web resources) to answer these questions factually instead of emotionally.
- One student should represent Washington, DC (taxation without representation).

## *Closure*

- Students meet as a simulated legislative body.
  - The teacher serves as chairperson and parliamentarian.
  - The goal is for the students to "pass" a federal tax bill that will be fair to the citizens and meet the needs of the people.
  - The students need to balance this bill across the states they represent (for instance, flood insurance for states on the coast or near large bodies of water), concerns for the environment (mountaintop mining, or drilling for gas/oil in Alaska, etc.).
- Students write an essay or journal entry explaining the functions of taxes and evaluating what they think is a "fair" system of taxation.

## Timing

- Depending on the students in the class and the subject (economics versus U.S. or world history) the time will vary. The lecture should take no longer than 30 minutes; 20 would be optimum. A note-taking guide could be posted on the chalkboard or overhead projector to help focus students on important information.
- After the lecture, the students could complete their research during that class period and part of the next.
- In a block schedule, they could complete their research in one day.
- The mini-Congress can be limited to 30 minutes, especially if the teacher has prepared a skeleton bill for the students to amend. If it is going well, the time can be extended.
- The essay/journal entry can be assigned as homework or as part of a unit test.

## Materials

- World Book General Information: http://www.worldbook.com/fun/taxation/html/major_types.htm
- Estate Taxes: http://www.mycounsel.com/content/estateplanning/deathandtaxes/types.html
- Graphic Organizer for Taxes: http://www.curriculumlink.org/econ/materials/taxtypes.html
- Types of Sales Tax: http://www.toolkit.cch.com/text/P07_4015.asp
- PowerPoint Types of Taxes: http://people.clemson.edu/~cl/Acct404/01/sld007.htm

# Production, Distribution, and Consumption

- CBS News Interactive: http://people.clemson.edu/~cl/Acct404/01/
- sld007.htm
- Recognize, Interpret, Manipulate Different Taxes: http://www.tomah.k12.wi.us/phoenix/Competency_1700.html
- Yahoo Search on Different Taxes: http://dir.yahoo.com/Government/U_S__Government/Taxes/
- Environmental Taxes: http://www.oecd.org/env/policies/taxes/
- Global Taxes: http://www.globalpolicy.org/socecon/glotax/
- E-taxes: http://fcw.com/civic/articles/2001/mar/civ-feature3-03-01.asp
- Study Web: Taxes around the World: http://www.studyWeb.com/links/108.html
- State and Local Taxes: http://www.ustreas.gov/opc/opc0078.html
- Purpose of Taxation: Federalist Papers: http://classicals.com/federalist/TheFederalisthall/messages/888.html
- History of U.S. Taxation: http://www.taxhistory.org/
- History of Economic Thought: http://taxes.about.com/money/taxes/cs/taxhistory/

# Evaluation Rubric

## Rubric for "Mini-Congress"

During the Congressional debate the student:

|  | Excellent | Very Good | Satisfactory | Needs Improvement |
|---|---|---|---|---|
| Demonstrated understanding of basic tax issues | Defines issues thoroughly with examples or illustrations | Defines issues clearly | Defines issues | Does not define issues |
| Demonstrated an understanding of the complexity of fair taxation | Explains complexity thoroughly with examples or illustrations | Some understanding of complexity of the word "fair" | Little understanding of complexity and few or no examples | No understanding of complexity. Example inappropriate or not used |
| Represented his/her assigned state/region of the country accurately | Represents the region accurately | Represents the region with minor errors or leaves out some points | Basically represents the region with errors or major points missing | Misrepresents the region. Makes errors |
| Cited evidence (facts) to back up opinions | Opinions fully backed with facts | Opinions backed with some facts | Opinions backed with at least one fact | Opinions not backed up with facts |
| Respected fellow Congressional Delegates (followed parliamentary procedure) | Thorough knowledge of parliamentary procedure | Some knowledge of parliamentary procedure but confused on the fine points | Little knowledge of fine points of parliamentary procedure | Cannot follow rules of parliamentary procedure |
| Spoke clearly and correctly (grammar and usage) | Speaks clearly and convincingly. Correct English usage | Speaks clearly; minor errors in English usage | Speech may be garbled. Errors in usage | Incoherent or confused. Major usage errors |

**Rubric for Essay:** Modify rubric for persuasive or position papers from "What Are My Rights?" lesson.

# Science, Technology, and Society

Because we live in the midst of a technological revolution, the importance of this theme—science, technology and society—is obvious. Yet, frequently, social studies/history teachers shy away from a discussion of the role of science and technology in history. This is true because teachers tend to feel insecure with topics for which they haven't had much academic preparation. Traditionally, teachers teach the Industrial Revolution or the Scientific Revolution as the names, inventions, and dates of the time period. The inclusion of the history of science and technology as a theme in social studies classes is a fairly recent occurrence.

Progress in science and technology has both enabled our modern lifestyle and brought us to the brink of annihilation. This theme enables students to explore the role of science and technology by using technology to do their research. How do science and technology affect the values and beliefs of society? How do human beings cope with the rate of change in our society? How can we manage our progress, instead of having our progress manage us?

Interdisciplinary work could focus on English class with reading of literature like Orwell's *1984*, or with science class, even by focusing on a classic like Carson's *Silent Spring*, which led to the banning of the pesticide DDT. Issues like cloning, biogenetic engineering of food, etc., fall within social studies and science curricula. Or, if the school has a junior ROTC program, here is a chance to incorporate the teacher of that course into the lesson on technology and weaponry.

The lessons in this section handle the theme very differently. The first lesson focuses on the technology of warfare. From the earliest recorded history, the side with the most advanced weaponry (technology) frequently has been the winner of wars that have changed our history. The lesson has been written to encompass both world history and U.S. history simply based on the teacher's decision of which wars to discuss.

The "update" of the lesson—to increase its relevance and meaning—is the discussion of the desire on the part of the present administration to revive the idea of a missile shield over the U.S. This requires unilateral abandonment of the ABM Treaty that is causing much concern among the other nations in the world. Additionally, reports on "smart bombs" and pinpoint bombing, coupled with special operations forces, fill the news as the current war against terrorism continues. Media reports discuss a new kind of war for a new kind of threat. Thus, students view the technology of war along a continuum from the past to the present.

The second lesson examines plagues and the spread of disease. The lesson focuses on the Black Plague in world history and the current AIDS crisis. Students are always fascinated with the Black Plague. This lesson incorporates map and graph analysis to enhance social studies skills. In addition, students are called upon to understand the social and economic impact of sickness.

An American history teacher can switch the topic of study to the influenza epidemic and AIDS. Influenza was, like the Black Plague and AIDS, a worldwide phenomenon. The lesson contains Web sites for information about all three plagues. Follow-up discussions could examine other current problems like cattle with foot and mouth disease, West Nile virus, smallpox and anthrax, etc. Through this lesson, students will become more aware of the global nature of their daily lives.

Science, Technology, and Society

# The Technology of Warfare

## NCSS Theme
### Science, Technology, and Society
"Examine and describe the influence of culture on scientific and technological choices and advancement, such as in transportation, medicine, and warfare."[a]

## Objectives
### Subject Area National Standard
History Standard 5: Historic Issues–Analysis and Decision Making.

### Skills Standards or Objectives
The student is able to:
"Identify causes of the problem or dilemma."[b]
"Propose alternative ways of resolving the problem or dilemma."[b]
"Formulate a position or course of action on an issue."[b]

### Attitude Standard or Objective
Students will appreciate the role that science and technology play in a country's safety and security.

[a] *Expectations of Excellence*, p. 99
[b] *National Standards for History*, p. 23

## Procedures
### Set
- Begin by discussing President G. W. Bush's call for a missile shield.
- Why does he want funds to try to design and build such a shield?
- Is this considered an "offensive" or a "defensive" move?
  - Help students to understand that what is "defensive" by one country may be considered "offensive" by another county if it negates the weapons of that country.
- Explain that this decision relates to unilateral abrogation of the ABM Treaty.
- Focus the discussion on the idea that controlling or winning a given area depends on having the most efficient weapons.
- Segue into the lesson on what history can teach us about the power of technology.

### Body of Lesson
This is an opportunity to look at a theme in history: technology and warfare, or, when teaching a particular time or war, to bring up the topic for a single lesson. Appropriate examples would include some of the following:

- Roman battle techniques during the Punic War when Roman soldiers, by using planks with grappling hooks that could latch on to enemy ships, created a flat fighting surface. The Romans were able to create "land" for an army on the sea.
- The Roman battle formations using their shields to form a "turtle" to cover their heads and their sides to enable the legion to move forward in an attack and still be protected.
- The invention of the longbow and its use during the Battle of Agincourt, the last British victory in the Hundred Year's War.
- The small, easily maneuverable British ships that were able to sink (with the help of the weather) the Spanish Armada. The army troops on the Armada ships never were able to reach the land to fight their battle.
- The ironclad ships of the U.S. Civil War.
- The invention of the repeating rifle (machine gun, etc.).
- Admiral Mahan's call to the U.S. to build a navy under the belief that the country that controlled the seas would control the world.
- The invention of the submarine.
- The invention of the airplane (who controls the skies, controls the world).
- The invention of the nuclear bomb, and, subsequently, ICBMs and SLBMs.
  - Thus the need for the shield to counteract the missiles (who controls space controls the world).

Suggestions for lessons include the movie *Henry V*, which demonstrates the power of the longbow.

- If the movie is too long, the teacher could combine forces with the English teacher and each could show half the movie.
- It is important when showing this movie that students be prepared for the Shakespearian language.
- In my experience, students begin to understand the language after approximately 15 minutes of the movie.
- Occasionally, the teacher needs to stop the movie and explain a point (for example, as the movie opens, the discussion of the law: the King of England believed he had a legitimate claim to the territory of France).
- If there is not enough time, then the scenes of the battle with the longbow arrows piercing the air and breaking the French ranks can be used alone.

To handle the topic thematically, the class could be broken into cooperative groups.

- Each group would be assigned a period in history where warfare was substantively changed as the result of a change in the technology of the weapons in use. Include a group on bioterrorism as a modern threat.
- The groups would report to the class in chronological order (either oral reports or multimedia presentations where pictures of the weapons could be included).

## Closure

For a thematic lesson, hold a class debate:
- ♦ Debate Resolution: Resolved that the Congress should allocate all funds requested for the research, development, and deployment of a defensive missile shield for the United States.
  - Students will debate the wisdom and feasibility of building a missile defense system for the United States.
  - They would need to discuss the history of technology in terms of national security, using specific examples from their historic research.
  - This debate should not focus on the cost of such a program and/or other things the money could be used to buy.
  - This debate is on the role of science and technology in defense of national interests.

For a single lesson, students will write an essay or journal entry explaining the role of science and technology in national security using the historic event(s) studied as an example(s).
- ♦ This essay should include a position statement on
  - Research
  - Development
  - Deployment of a defensive missile shield for the United States
  - The cost to the U.S. politically

## Timing

This lesson could take as little as one class period, with the essay assigned for homework, or could be stretched into a short (one week) thematic unit. The lesson would also make a nice thematic review of wars studied across the school term.

## Materials

History textbooks
Information on technology and war
- ♦ http://Web.uvic.ca/shakespeare/Library/SLTnoframes/history/warfare.html
- ♦ http://www.loyola.edu/dept/philosophy/techne/techwar.htm
- ♦ http://www.ghsteched.com/warfare.html
- ♦ http://www.acq.osd.mil/ousda/speech/norfolknato.html
- ♦ http://www.columbia.edu/~mrg24/warintro.html
- ♦ http://www.thinkquest.org/library/lib/site_sum_outside.html?tname=16650&url=16650/cann_r2.htm
- ♦ http://www.idsa-india.org/an-apr9-9.html
- ♦ http://www.fiu.edu/~eltonh/warfare/rwarfare.html
- ♦ http://departments.colgate.edu/peacestudies/core310/technology.htm
- ♦ http://victorian.fortunecity.com/benjamin/440/

- http://www.lcss.net/num/exhibits.htm
- http://militaryhistory.about.com/mbody.htm
- http://cal044202.student.utwente.nl/~marsares/warfare/history/megiddo.html
- http://memory.loc.gov/

Recent newspaper, magazine or Web site discussions of President G.W. Bush's requests for a missile shield system.

- http://www.nytimes.com/2001/04/30/world/30MISS.html
- http://www.cnn.com/2001/WORLD/europe/06/13/russia.bush/
- http://www.space.com/spacenews/spacepolicy/missile_defense_speech_010501.html
- http://www.newsmax.com/archives/articles/2001/6/6/145859.shtml
- http://www.washingtonpost.com/ac2/wp-dyn/A29775-2001May1?language=printer

# Science, Technology, and Society

# Evaluation Rubric

For either a debate or a position paper:

|  | A<br>*Excellent* | B<br>*Very good* | C<br>*Acceptable* | D<br>*Unacceptable* |
|---|---|---|---|---|
| Student must take either the affirmative or the negative position | Student takes a firm position | Student states a position but is less sure of this stand | Student discusses issue but takes no position | Neither a discussion of the issue nor a position |
| Student backs up opinion with facts | Substantial factual evidence backs opinions | Some factual evidence backs opinions | Little factual evidence backs opinions | Very little to no factual evidence presented |
| Student cites sources for facts | Citations are complete | Sources are mentioned but may have minor errors | Some sources are cited | Little to no mention of sources for facts |
| Student is aware of the arguments of the opposing position and answers them in his/her statement | Student presents all arguments for and against his/her position | Student presents most arguments for and against his/her position | Student presents at least some argument for or against his/her position. Arguments may be lopsided | Little to no argument presented. Student is unaware that there are two sides to the argument |
| Student speaks (writes) clearly and concisely | Well written and well delivered | Student speaks and writes fairly well | Student has some difficulty writing and speaking clearly and concisely | Student is neither clear nor concise |
| Grammar and usage | Grammar and usage are correct | Minor errors in grammar and usage may be present | Grammar and usage are generally acceptable | Grammar and usage are unacceptable |

Comments:

Final project grade:

# Epidemics Then and Now: The Plague and AIDS

## NCSS Theme
### Science, Technology and Society

"Identify and describe both current and historical examples of the interaction and interdependence of science, technology, and society in a variety of cultural settings."[a]

"Recognize and interpret varied perspectives about human societies and the physical world using scientific knowledge, ethical standards, and technologies from diverse world cultures."[a]

## Objectives
### Subject Area National Standards

World History Standard Era 5, Standard 5, "Patterns of Crisis and Recovery in Afro-Eurasia 1300-1450."[b]

Standard 5A. "Demonstrate understanding of the Black Death and recurring plague pandemic in the 14th century."[b]

### Skills Standards or Objectives

"Explaining the origins and characteristics of the plague pandemic of the mid-14th century, and describing its spread across Eurasia and North Africa [reconstruct patterns of historic succession and duration]."[b]

"Analyzing the demographic, economic, social and political effects of the plague pandemic …[evidence historic perspectives]."[b]

"Assessing ways in which long-term climatic change contributed to Europe's economic and social crisis in the 14th century [interrogate historic data]."[b]

### Attitude Standards or Objectives

Understand the causes of the AIDS epidemic and the usefulness of science to blocking its spread and finding a cure.

Students will be able to compare and contrast two pandemics including the reactions and beliefs of the general population when threatened with terminal illnesses.

[a] *Expectations of Excellence, p. 132*
[b] *National Standards for World History, p. 154*

## Procedures
### Set

- Ask the class:
  - How many of you have ever heard of AIDS (Acquired Immune Deficiency Syndrome)?
  - What is AIDS?

# Science, Technology, and Society

- What is AIDS?
- How is AIDS transmitted, etc.?
- Has anyone heard of the word "epidemic"?
- How about "pandemic"?

The purpose of this short discussion is to get the students to think about the concepts of epidemics and pandemics.

- ♦ Have the students write down the definitions of AIDS, epidemic, and pandemic in their notebooks.
  - AIDS: Acquired Immune Deficiency Syndrome, a disease that weakens the immune system leading to complications and, usually, death. AIDS is caused by a retrovirus and is spread primarily through blood and blood products by entering the body's bloodstream (generally through either sexual contact and/or hypodermic needles).
  - Epidemic: A rapid increase in the spread of something. In the case of a disease, the rapid spread amongst the population of a disease that was previously not widespread or permanently prevalent.
  - Pandemic: A disease prevalent throughout an entire country, continent, or the whole world.

## Body of Lesson

- ♦ The purpose of the lesson is to have the students research the Black Death and AIDS by constructing a compare/contrast chart that will lead them to deeper understandings of:
  - How the general population responded during each epidemic.
  - The scientific explanations that will help protect people from these diseases (the plague still exists).
  - The role citizens can play in preventing the spread of disease.
  - The responsibilities citizens have to help people and countries where disease is widespread.
- ♦ In addition, students can create maps and graphs demonstrating the spread of the two epidemics to give them practice with interpreting maps and graphs.
- ♦ It is important that students focus on the political, social, economic and religious aspects of reactions to and effects of these plagues.
  - For example, during the Black Death in Europe, Jews were often used as scapegoats and were persecuted because people believed that they caused the disease.
  - In America, AIDS was initially labeled a "gay" disease, and homosexuals were shunned and their lifestyle blamed for the illness and its spread.
  - Thus, for both religious and political reasons, anti-Semitism increased in Europe, and, in terms of AIDS, research and support was initially hard to fund in the U.S. and still faces resistance in certain areas (sex education in schools that would teach AIDS prevention beyond abstinence).

## Closure

- Students will write an essay (they may do this "open note" using the charts if the teacher wishes) comparing and contrasting the two epidemics.
- This essay needs to include recommendations for action by the U.S. and/or the U.N. (United Nations) to:
  - Help contain the spread of AIDS
  - Help those nations suffering from widespread AIDS
  - Provide ideas for how science and technology can help with this problem

## Timing

Timing will vary depending on how much time the teacher wishes to devote to this area. If time is short, focus on the compare-and-contrast chart. If there is more time, the teacher might have students either create maps and graphs demonstrating the spread of the disease or simply access maps from Web sites below and have students interpret them. This is an opportunity to use social studies data (maps, graphs, charts) to demonstrate the spread of a problem throughout the world.

## Materials

Below is a partial list of the many Web sites available to help the teacher and the student access information about the two pandemics.

**Black Death Links**

- http://www.byu.edu/ipt/projects/middleages/LifeTimes/Plague.html
- http://www.discovery.com/stories/history/blackdeath/blackdeath.html
- http://users.netaccess.co.nz/chocfish/histpage_bd.html
- http://www.insecta-inspecta.com/fleas/bdeath/
- http://bw.k12.ri.us/Kicke/middleages%5Cplague.htm
- http://limiting.tripod.com/bd.htm
- http://www.bbc.co.uk/education/medicine/nonint/middle/dt/madtcs1.shtml
- http://www.fordham.edu/halsall/jewish/1348-jewsblackdeath.html
- http://www.history-magazine.com/black.html
- http://www.ucalgary.ca/HIST/tutor/endmiddle/bluedot/blackdeath.html

**AIDS Epidemic Links**

- http://www.fhi.org/en/aids/impact/mapgva.html
- http://www.un.org/womenwatch/daw/csw/hivaids/
- http://www.usnews.com/usnews/issue/000724/aids.htm
- http://www.utexas.edu/ftp/depts/systbiol/44_1/mindell/mindell.html
- http://allafrica.com/stories/200105070447.html
- http://www.advocatesforyouth.org/publications/factsheet/fshivaidsaf.htm

# Science, Technology, and Society

- http://www.cnn.com/2000/US/04/30/aids.threat.02/
- http://news.crosswalk.com/religion/item/0,1875,344924,00.htm
- http://www.hiv-development.org/se/publications/FROM%20AIDS%20EPIDEMICS%20TO%20AN%20AIDS%20PANDEMIC.asp
- http://seattletimes.nwsource.com/news/nation-world/html98/aids30_20000430.html
- http://www.datalounge.com/datalounge/news/record.html?record=4906

**For U.S. History Class: Influenza Links**
- http://www.stanford.edu/group/virus/uda/
- http://www.spartacus.schoolnet.co.uk/FWWinfluenzia.htm
- http://www.hi.is/~sigrug/
- http://dir.yahoo.com/Arts/Humanities/History/By_Time_Period/20th_Century/1918_Influenza_Pandemic/
- http://www.rbls.lib.il.us/dpl/HIDinfluenz.htm
- http://www.acsu.buffalo.edu/~mcoates/flu.htm
- http://www.ukans.edu/~kansite/ww_one/medical/mja.htm
- http://www.bath.ac.uk/~ma0pmf/1918Pandemic.html
- http://www.medicalpost.com/mdlink/english/members/medpost/data/3512/09A.HTM
- http://www.roangelo.net/schlectweg/influenz.html

**Is Influenza Still a Threat Today?**
- http://www.cia.gov/cia/publications/nie/report/nie99-17d.html
- http://www.killerplagues.com/mlinks.html
- http://www.cdc.gov/ncidod/diseases/flu/fluvirus.htm
- http://www.who.int/inf-fs/en/fact211.html
- http://www.disasterrelief.org/Disasters/990222Flu2/index_txt.html
- http://144.92.49.74:81/ScienceEd/stories/storyReader$47
- http://www.naturejpn.com/newnature/bionews/bionews000517/bionewse-000517e.htm
- http://www.junkscience.com/news/fluprimr.htm

Check the fall 2001 newspaper indexes for the *New York Times* (http://www.nytimes.com) and the *Washington Post;* they have run major series on hoof and mouth disease, AIDS, anthrax, and smallpox. In addition, in response to current events, the fall 2001 newspapers ran updated information on influenza to induce people to get a flu shot for the winter 2001/2002 flu season.

# Evaluation Rubric

This chart is set up as a worksheet/rubric for the basic (lower-ability level) student. There is a single column for similar or different. A general student could use two columns to compare and contrast to show a more complex answer. An advanced student could add a column for current disease threats (including bioterrorism).

|  | *Black Death* | *AIDS* | *Similar/ Different* | *Points Awarded* |
|---|---|---|---|---|
| Cause of disease |  |  |  |  |
|  |  |  |  |  |
| Symptoms of disease |  |  |  |  |
|  |  |  |  |  |
| Spread by? |  |  |  |  |
|  |  |  |  |  |
| Number of people affected? |  |  |  |  |
|  |  |  |  |  |
| Locations affected? |  |  |  |  |
|  |  |  |  |  |
| Economic impact? |  |  |  |  |
|  |  |  |  |  |
| Religious reactions (response)? |  |  |  |  |
|  |  |  |  |  |
| Political response? |  |  |  |  |
|  |  |  |  |  |
| Social impact? |  |  |  |  |
|  |  |  |  |  |
| Scientific knowledge for prevention? |  |  |  |  |
|  |  |  |  |  |
| **Total points** |  |  |  |  |

**Summary:**
Write a statement comparing and contrasting the Black Death and AIDS.

# Global Connections

A person can hardly turn on the television news or read a newspaper without confronting the reality of our global interdependence. Our technology has enabled us to trade with, visit, communicate with, and be a part of nations all over the globe. We hear about the global village. We are warned by some of the dangers of unitary world government and by others of the promise of that same concept: unitary world government. The closer we get to each other, the further apart our social, ethnic, racial, and religious differences seem to drive us. This theme, global connections, addresses issues of the commonalities and the needs of humans around the world. The focus is on traditional political and economic history, as well as on newer social and ethical considerations.

What are our obligations to our fellow humans? In addition to the social studies areas of geography, history and economics, this theme lends itself well to reaching out with a service learning program. Another approach is the utilization of communications software to enable students to meet other persons in foreign lands, for example, "e-pals."

The first lesson in this section provides a mechanism for teachers to tie their world history course together at the end of the term. By focusing on the application of concepts and facts, students get to cement their learning in a review that is more meaningful than memorizing material for the final exam. This assignment familiarizes students with the connections between our current problems and the history that preceded them. Students should enjoy using what they learned to bring understanding to the world in which they live.

The second lesson focuses on emerging global issues. Students will use the Internet to search for problems, treaties, analyses, interest groups, etc., that deal with defense, the environment, population problems, conflict resolution, etc. Because this lesson was designed prior to September 11, 2001, it included terrorism as a topic for investigation. In light of recent events, some teachers might want to teach terrorism as an independent topic and remove it as a topic for this lesson. The lesson applies to any social studies course, depending on the issues covered. The objectives used are aimed at world and contemporary U.S. history. Comparative government would also be an appropriate course for this lesson.

Both of these lessons focus students on researching current events issues to create understanding about the world in which they live. Whether students do this research using the Internet or newspapers and magazines from the school media center/library, the goal is to help history live by connecting the past to the present and the future.

# Reviewing World History Concepts

## NCSS Theme
### Global Connections

"Social studies programs should include experiences that provide for the study of *global connections* and *interdependence*."[a]

## Objectives
### Subject Area National Standards

World History Standard 2: "Historic Comprehension."[b]

World History Standard 5. A.: "Students should be able to 'identify issues and problems in the past.'"[c]

### Skills Standard or Objective

World History Standard 3. J.: "Students should be able to hypothesize the influence of the past."[c]

### Attitude Standard or Objective

World History Standards' general aim: understanding or the integration of historic thinking and historic understanding.

[a] *Expectations of Excellence*, p. 136
[b] *National Standards for World History*, p. 18
[c] p. 19

## Procedures
### Set

- Ask students how many read either the newspaper or a news magazine (*Newsweek, Time, U.S. News and World Reports*) on a regular basis?
- Why or why not?
- What can you learn from these publications?
- Are there differences among magazines and newspapers?
- If yes, what are the differences? (Teacher is checking to make sure students are aware of political bias, etc.)

As a review at the end of the course, we are going to work on the following project:

### Body of Lesson

Distribute the assignment sheet that begins on the next page.

# Current Events/ Classifying Information

Date Due: _____ (No late projects, even for excused absence, without telephone contact from parent/guardian).

## Introduction

This year we have been separating the information into each of the following categories (PERSIA):

- Political
- Economic
- Religious
- Social
- Intellectual
- Aesthetic
- In some cases, we added "military" and/or "decline."

We used these categories to analyze the topic we were studying and to explain the factors that had the most effect at any given time. These are standard areas of study for social scientists, and you need to be able to separate them in order to understand historic events.

## Assignment

- You will compile a current events notebook that will contain approximately 12 to 14 articles.
- These articles must be separated (classified) according to the type of information you wish the article to convey.
- The written explanation accompanying the article will explain how the article fits the category chosen.
- You must include two (2) articles/category (total of 12 articles).
- Extra Credit: you may chose to submit two (2) extra articles for a non-required seventh category, either "military" or "decline."

## Procedure

- Select articles from newspapers and/or magazines during the next month.
  - If you are not allowed to cut these articles out, you may submit copies of them instead of originals (be sure to note that the information was from a library or that your parents did not want the material cut up).
  - All the articles must deal with foreign (non-U.S.) countries. This is because you are concentrating on world history this year.
  - The greater the spread of subjects (more countries covering wider geographical locations) the more interesting your project will be.
- Mount each article on a sheet of paper.

- Underline or highlight the information that relates to the category for which you are using it.
  - For example, underline only the information pertaining to religion if the article is explaining religious factors.
- Write a short explanation (no more than one paragraph) on the importance of the article in relation to the category.
  - If the article is about Buddhism and burial customs of the Chinese make sure you write that Buddhism is a religion we studied and explain why this is important to our understanding of the modern Chinese.
♦ I am looking for an integration of the understanding of the concepts we have studied and of the impact these concepts have on the modern world.
♦ The finished project should display your ability to:
  - Classify information.
  - Explain its importance both in history and today.
♦ BE SURE TO INCLUDE A COMPLETE CITATION FOR EACH ARTICLE!

## *Miscellaneous*

♦ Remember that each category includes many concepts, for example:
  - Political: democracy, socialism, communism, natural rights, etc.
  - Economic: recession, depression, inflation, capitalism, communism, etc.
  - Religious: Islam, Judaism, Christianity, Hinduism; freedom to worship, etc.
  - Social: class structure, education, drug abuse, health, civil rights, etc.
  - Intellectual: philosophy, ideas, writings behind government, law, ethics, etc.
  - Aesthetic: art, music, dance of a country.
♦ It should be obvious that several concepts can cross categories, e.g., communism. This requires you to explain the context of your example.
♦ The extra credit category is either "military" or "decline." If you find articles relating to the warfare or decline of a modern nation, you may use them in this area.

## *Grading*

The project will be graded according to a chart that will encompass:
♦ Two articles/categories
♦ Good choice of articles
♦ Spread of topics
♦ Good and varied sources
♦ Well underlined/highlighted
♦ Short, concise explanation linking article to topics studied
♦ Correct citations

- Neatness
- Grammar
- Spelling
- Overall organization of the current events notebook

## Timing

- This assignment is set up as a grading period homework project.
- To do this in class, decide how many factors (just political, economic, and social, or all factors) you wish to use.
- If students have no access to newspapers, usually upon request the local newspaper will supply papers to the classroom for a limited (one to two weeks) period of time.
- An additional source of articles would be the newspaper "online," accessed either in the classroom or through the school media center.

## Materials

- Newspapers and/or weekly news magazines
- This is an opportunity to introduce some magazines students may not have seen, e.g., *New Republic*, *National Review*, *Atlantic Monthly*, the *Nation*, etc., in addition to the traditional ones
- Highlighters for underlining
- Paper for mounting articles
- Glue or tape for mounting
- Folder or small notebook for compiling articles
- Copies of the assignment sheet and the evaluation rubric

# Evaluation Rubric
## Current Events/PERSIA Project Rubric

| Article | (1)<br>PERSIA Category | (1)<br>Underline | (3)<br>Explanation | (1)<br>Source | Total |
|---|---|---|---|---|---|
| 1. | | | | | |
| 2. | | | | | |
| 3. | | | | | |
| 4. | | | | | |
| 5. | | | | | |
| 6. | | | | | |
| 7. | | | | | |
| 8. | | | | | |
| 9. | | | | | |
| 10. | | | | | |
| 11. | | | | | |
| 12. | | | | | (72) |
| Extra Credit | | | | | (12) |
| 13. | | | | | |
| 14. | | | | | |
| | | | | | |
| | | (3) | Organization | | |
| | | (5) | Citations | | |
| | | (5) | Neatness | | |
| | | (5) | Spelling | | |
| | | (5) | Grammar | | |
| | | (28) | | | |
| | | | | Total Grade | |

Comments:

# A Global Village?

## NCSS Theme
### Global Connections

"Social studies programs should include experiences that provide for the study of *global connections* and *interdependence*."[a]

"Analyze the causes, consequences, and possible solutions to persistent, contemporary, and emerging global issues, such as health, security, resource allocation, economic development, and environmental quality."[a]

"Analyze the relationships and tensions between national sovereignty and global interests in matters such as territory, economic development, nuclear and other weapons, use of natural resources, and human rights concerns."[a]

## Objectives
### Subject Area National Standards

U.S. History: Era 10: Contemporary United States.
Standard 1: "Recent developments in foreign policy and domestic politics."[b]
Standard 1C: "The student understands major foreign policy initiatives."[b]

### Skills Standards or Objectives

"The student is able to evaluate the reformulation of foreign policy in the post-Cold War era [analyze cause and effect]."[b]

World History: Era 8: the 20th Century:
Standard 6E: "Assessing the impact of space explorations, biotechnology, the new physics, and medical advances on human society and ecology."[c]

"Analyzing how revolutions in communications, information technology and mass marketing techniques have contributed to the acceleration of social change and the rise of a 'global culture' [analyze multiple causation]."[c]

### Attitude Standard or Objective

Students will appreciate that they are citizens of the world.

[a] *Expectations of Excellence*, p. 136
[b] *National Standards for World History*, p. 128
[c] *National Standards for World History*, p. 282

## Procedures
### Set

- Ask students to define the word "treaty."
  - "A treaty is an agreement between two or more nations in reference to peace, alliance, commerce, or other international relations. A formal document embodying such agreement" (*Random House Dictionary of the English Language*).

- Prepare a blank bulletin board by tacking up background paper and the letters to form the words "Global Issues," or "Global Problems," "Global Concerns," etc. (leave the rest of the space open for the students to fill in with pictures and written documents).
- The purpose of our lesson will be to select several issues of world importance and research them. Hopefully the class will come away with opinions on how our political representatives should deal with these topics as they come up for discussion in the Congress.

## *Body of Lesson*

- Have students brainstorm the "global issues" of the day. List their issues on the chalkboard.
- Try to steer students towards issues where there are international treaties or signed documents that the U.S. has (or in some cases, has not) signed.
- These issues might include, but are not limited to:
  - World trade
  - The environment
  - Global warming
  - Sharing the oceans and seas
  - Scientific research (space exploration, cloning, stem-cell research, etc.)
  - World health
  - Genocide
  - Drugs
  - Defense
  - Women's rights
  - Terrorism
  - Copyright laws (or bootlegging of movies and music)
- Divide students into groups by their interest in specific issues. This is most fairly done by having students select their top three issues, writing them on a slip of paper, and handing them to the teacher for sorting. There should be no discussion among students when selecting issues (this will prevent friends from "stacking" the groups).
- Each group will work in the library/media center researching information on their issue.
- The groups will prepare a short presentation for the class on their issue. Each presentation should:
  - Define the underlying problem or issue.
  - Explain the different positions taken by the U.S., its allies, other nations, nongovernmental organizations (NGOs or interest groups).
  - Enumerate potential solutions to the problems/issue.
  - Lead the class in a short discussion of the issue.
  - Explain what the group thinks the best solution might be or guide the class to reach a consensus solution.

- Prepare information to be included on a bulletin board entitled: "Global Issues."
- Students take notes on issues during presentations.

## *Closure*

- Students make their presentations to the class. PowerPoint, Hyperstudio, or ClarisWorks are the preferred format.
- Students add the appropriate bulletin board section to the prepared bulletin board space.
- Students write a journal entry briefly outlining each issue presented and their feelings about the problem.

## **Timing**

- Students will need at least one regular-period day to do the research.
- Students need one period to design and prepare their presentation and bulletin board section.
- Students need one to two periods (or more) to discuss the issues.
- The time is dependent on:
  - How long the teacher wishes to give each group to present.
  - How much discussion is desired.
  - How many issues will be covered.

## **Materials**

Sources for some of the most important issues are below:

**Treaties and International Agreements**

- World Treaties: http://www.123world.com/worldtreaties/
- World Constitutions and Treaties: http://library.tamu.edu/govdocs/workshop/
- Council for a Livable World: http://www.clw.org/
- Worldwatch: http://www.worldwatch.org/
- Fourth World Documentation Project: http://www.cwis.org/fwdp/fwdp.html
- International Topics and Issues, U.S. Dept. of State: http://www.state.gov/interntl/
  - http://www.willamette.edu/law/longlib/forint.htm
  - http://www.lib.uchicago.edu/~llou/forintlaw.html

**Defense**

- http://www.ukdf.org.uk/gr45.htm
- NATO: http://www.nato.int/home.htm
- Peace, Conflict Resolution and International Security: http://www.etown.edu/vl/peace.html

- Center for Missile Defense: http://www.cdi.org/hotspots/missiledefense/

**Environmental Treaties**
- http://environment.harvard.edu/guides/intenvpol/resources/BJC6161_Maffei_world_treaty_data.html
- Kyoto treaty: @D33 = http://www.cnn.com/SPECIALS/1997/global.warming/stories/treaty/
- http://www.oneworld.org/ips2/dec/kyoto_12.html
- http://www.newsmax.com/archives/articles/2001/3/29/164418.shtml

**Law of the Sea**
- http://www.un.org/Depts/los/index.htm
- http://www.state.gov/www/global/oes/oceans/980610_los.html
- http://www.greenpeace.org/~intlaw/lsconts.html

**Intellectual Property**
- http://www.wipo.int/treaties/index.html

**Universal Declaration of Human Rights**
- http://www.psr.keele.ac.uk/const.htm

**Trade**
- http://www.natlaw.com/treaties.htm
- http://www.fas.usda.gov/info/factsheets/wto.html
- World Trade Organization: http://amsterdam.nettime.org/Lists-Archives/nettime-l-0001/msg00096.html
- http://www.dfait-maeci.gc.ca/tna-nac/list-e.asp
- http://www.wtowatch.org/
- History of: http://www.arches.uga.edu/~cowgill/_trade/node25.html

**Health Treaties**
- http://www.who.int/inf-pr-2001/en/pr2001WHA-6.html
- http://www.yale.edu/lawWeb/avalon/decade/decad051.htm
- Framework convention on tobacco: http://sftfc.globalink.org/whatisfctc.html
- Drug Policy: http://www.haiWeb.org/campaign/access/wha54/briefingen.html

# Evaluation Rubric

|  | Outstanding | Very Good | Satisfactory | Needs Improvement |
|---|---|---|---|---|
| Defined the problem or issue | Clear, concise explanation that was easy for the class to understand | Clear explanation that the class could understand | Explanation that gave the class a basic knowledge of the issue | Not informative about the issue, confusing, unclear |
| Explained different positions | Accounted for complexity among multiple interest groups | Accounted for some multiple perspectives | Mentioned disagreements, explained at least two positions | Did not communicate complexity of the issue |
| Enumerated potential solutions | Accounted for several solutions including NGOs, governments, the U.N. | Accounted for multiple solutions but may not cover the entire range of possibilities | Listed two or more solutions but may be unsure why groups take the position that they do | Does not give potential solutions |
| Led the class in discussion of the issue | Posed effective questions, monitored discussion, stayed on topic | Discussion lagged a little but did cover the issue; basically stayed on topic. | Minimal discussion, questions less effective, strayed off topic at times | No prepared questions, little discussion, off topic |
| Suggested the best solution | Reached consensus | Agreed to disagree | Could not offer a compromise | No solution offered |
| Bulletin board information | Attractive, graphics and text, covered the issue | Graphic and text, covered the basic issue | Fewer artifacts, explained issue but not thoroughly | Minimal graphics or text documents, issue unclear |
| Group skills | Worked very well, whole group participated | Worked well, almost all students participated | Work was satisfactory, fewer participated | Work was poorly done, one or two students did all the work |
|  |  |  | Total Grade |  |
| Comments: |  |  |  |  |

# Civic Ideals and Practices

At its heart, the purpose of teaching and learning social studies/history is to enhance effective citizenship in our students. This was true when, in 1895, the Committee of Ten first mandated the study of history in the schools, and when the National Council for the Social Studies was chartered as part of the American Historical Association in 1921. From the era of Thomas Jefferson until today, our leaders and educators have understood that it will be the next generation that preserves and furthers our democracy. Despite our increasingly individualistic focus in this country, students must understand both the rights and the responsibilities inherent in democratic citizenship.

What is the role of the citizen in his or her local community, state, country, and world? Which causes are so worth preserving that a person would die to defend them? When should a citizen take a stand, and pay the price for, refusing to serve their government's demands? This theme cuts across most of the social studies areas but is especially relevant in history, government, civics, and law studies.

Here is a chance to team with the business department to discuss civic virtues in business or free market environments. This theme also provides focus for service learning, or co-curricular activities takes in student government, clubs, or team work/leadership.

Both lessons in this section focus on the civics/government standards. However, the lessons are easily adapted for U.S. history at the time students are working on elections, the Constitution, and/or the rights and responsibilities of citizens. The first lesson, "Unfair," zeroes in on a topic that most teenagers consider a "right" and most adults consider a "privilege." Although the issue in the lesson is the age and requirements for learner's permits and driving licenses, other topics, e.g., teenage curfews, could work equally well. This lesson is an example of how the government affects the lives of its citizens on a daily basis, an important concept for students to consider.

The second lesson is geared to the complaint by students about how boring elections are. Or, how there are no differences between the major political parties and, thus, no real choices. By studying third parties, students have the opportunity to explore issues from multiple perspectives. After completing this research, students might become more aware of why the differences between the two major parties seem minute. This exploration of differences in parties will assist students in understanding their feelings on the major issues of the day. This may help them become interested in political campaigns and in voting.

## Unfair?

### NCSS Theme
*Civic Ideals and Practices*[a]

Overlapping themes: Power, Authority, and Governance: Individuals, Groups, and Institutions

### Objectives
*Subject Area National Standard*

"How does the American political system provide for choice and opportunities for participation?"[b]

Era 10, 2E: "The student understands how a democratic polity debates social issues and mediates between individual or group rights and the common good."[c]

*Skills Standard or Objective*

"Locate, access, analyze, organize, synthesize, evaluate, and apply information about selected public issues: identifying, describing and evaluating multiple points of view."[c]

*Attitude Standard or Objective*

"Participate in activities to strengthen the 'common good,' based upon careful evaluation of possible options for citizen action."[c]

[a] *Expectations of Excellence*, p. 139
[b] *National Standards for Civics and Government*, p. 103
[c] *National Standards for History*, p. 130

Note: This lesson is based on the Jurisprudential Model of Teaching. This instructional strategy uses a legalistic or trial based approach to studying a public issue or controversy. Students may engage in Socratic discussion, a debate, or a simulated trial as the performance outcome for a lesson utilizing the Jurisprudential instructional model. The technology integration for this lesson includes online research and e-mail to legislators.

### Content Outline

- First, select a public policy issue that has high interest to students and is currently under discussion by the state or national legislature.
- This is most easily accomplished either through reading a daily newspaper or by reviewing the bills under legislative consideration on a state or federal government Web site.
- For this lesson, the topic of restrictions on teenage driving is appropriate because the issue has high interest for high school students and could be a topic that would propel them into action in terms of exercising their right to communicate their feelings on a public policy issue to their legislators.

- "Resolved: the Virginia legislature should pass legislation, SB 1330 and SB 1329, restricting the rights of teenager drivers." (2001)
  - SB 1330 would require that the age for obtaining a driver's license be increased from 16 to 16.6 years of age and raises the age for a learner's permit from 15 to 15.6.
  - SB 1329 would require issuance of provisional licenses to persons less than 18 years of age. This bill would prohibit persons under 18 from operating a motor vehicle with more than one teen passenger for the first six months of provisional licensure, or more than two teen passengers the second six months. Exception is made for members of the driver's family. Additionally, in order to obtain a driver's license, the learner's permit would be required, as would at least 40 hours of supervised driving including at least 10 hours between sunset and 10:00 P.M..
  - Further, there is legislation pending that would prohibit drivers under 18 from driving between the hours of midnight and 5:00 a.m. except for school- and job-related trips, for emergencies, or in the company of an adult.
- Students will be provided with Oliver and Shaver's "American Creed" document outlining fundamental beliefs about the rights of Americans in a democratic society.
  - Students will be provided with a series of articles from current newspapers discussing the move by the legislature to limit rights of teenage drivers.
  - Teenagers are thus defined as a "special class" both in need of protection from themselves and for the safety of the community (common good).
  - Social science statistics (rates of accidents, ages of drivers) from several states are included in the material.
  - The provisions of a "graduated license" for driving are included, as are comments from teenagers and parents.
  - An Internet connection in the classroom or library would be useful for more in-depth research.

## Procedures

### Set

- Who remembers the phrase that is carved into the frieze of the Supreme Court Building? *Equal justice under law.*
- Do all members of our society have equal protection under the law? *Various answers; probe with "why or why not?"*
- When does the state have the right to designate a "special group" and restrict their rights?
  - For example: Should teenagers have curfews imposed by the local or state government?

- Hold a brief discussion.

Teacher continues: "Today, as we continue our state government and public policy unit, we want to explore a current issue under consideration in our state legislature and our right as citizens to influence the outcome of that public policy debate."

- Your job during this class is to keep an open mind as we discuss/debate the issue.
- At the end of the class, you will be required to write a letter in the form of an e-mail to your state legislator communicating your position and trying to influence his/her vote on the issue.

## Body of Lesson

All statements are addressed from the teacher to the students:

- First, we will work in pairs discussing the issue of restrictions on teenage drivers and your feelings about this proposed legislation.
- You will need to work quickly, reviewing (sharing) the documents I have downloaded and sharing the Internet connection for research.
- At the end of the research period, you and your partner must be ready to take opposite sides of the issue (one for and one against the legislation).
- In this way, half the class will support and half the class will oppose these proposed Senate bills.
- You will note that several states in addition to Virginia are considering, or have adopted, driving restrictions for teenagers.
- This data from other states should help you formulate your argument as well as understand the concept of reserved powers.
  - Each state is on its own on this issue, but drivers cross state lines frequently; will the laws apply if you go from Virginia to Washington, DC or Maryland?
- Following the research period, we will discuss the issue.
- Remember our rules for Socratic discussion and our rules for debate:
  - Respect classmates
  - Back opinions with evidence
  - Keep an open mind
  - Define the problem
  - Look for multiple solutions, etc.
- I will intervene only if necessary to keep the discussion moving forward.

Note: This could be set up as a formal debate with assigned sides, or as a trial (of a juvenile who "broke" the law [once it was passed] and was trying to get the law declared unconstitutional).

## Closure

- We will each write a one-page summary of the issue in the form of a letter to be e-mailed (as a class digest) to our state senators and representatives with your opinions on how your legislators should vote on these issues.

- At this point, you may take either position (for or against) on these bills.
- If opposed to the bills, you need to offer alternative solutions to the problem of the high accident rate of teenage drivers.

## Timing

- This lesson can take as little as one single period, one block period, or be expanded to a larger research and writing project.
- If using only one period, the teacher would need to have downloaded and collected documents for the students to use in their pair research.
- If a longer time is allotted, students could do all the research themselves.

## Materials

A sample of materials on this issue, easily obtained from an online search and download of articles, is:

- *Mims Teen Driving Bills Find Local Support* http://leesburg2day.com/current.cfm?catid=54&newsid=2570
- *Metro Teens Have Mixed Reactions to Barnes' Driving Proposals* http://www.accessatlanta.com/partners/ajc/newsatlanta/ teens2001/010601.html
- *Readers Speak Out on Teen Driving and How to Make it Safer* http://www.acessatlanta.com/partnerns/ajc.newsatlanta/ teens2001/120700.html
- *Dept. of Highway Safety and Motor Vehicles: State of Florida* http:// www.hsmv.state.fl.us/news/newsteen.html
- *Teen Driving Laws Should Include All 159 Counties* http://www.acessatlanta.com/partnerns/ajc.newsatlanta/teens2001/edit0111.html
- *Bid to Raise Driving Age is Roiling Rural Georgia* http://www.nytimes.com/2001/01/14/national/14DRIV.html
- www.dcwatch.com/archives/council12/12-818.htm
- http://www.nhtsa.gov/people/injury/newdriver/saveteens/sect5.html
- http://www.cdc.gov/ncipc/factsheets/teenmvh.htm
- http://www.wvsafety.org/teendriving.htm
- http://www.safewaydriving.com/law.htm
- http://www.safewaydriving.com/law.htm

Oliver, D.W. and Shaver, J.P. (1966). *Teaching public issues in the high school.* Boston: Houghton Mifflin. "The American Creed" (this document lists basic beliefs and rights of Americans).

Teachers may access more material on the Jurisprudential Model of Teaching in Joyce, B. R. and Weil, M. (2000). *Models of teaching (6th ed.).* Boston: Allyn and Bacon.

# Evaluation Rubric

Students will be assessed on research and discussion skills using the rubric for grading (modified) from the Internet: http://education.nebrweslyan.edu/mcdonald/235Website/Model_Evals/JUR.html

E-mail letter will be graded in terms of:
- Taking a position on all parts of this legislation.
  - Driver's license age
  - Learner's permit age
  - Learner's permit hour requirements
  - Provisional license passenger restrictions
  - Curfew
- Defending the position with evidence (statistics, comments from insurance experts, psychologists, etc.).
- If opposed to the legislation (or any section thereof), providing an alternate solution to the problem.

## A, Excellent
- The student took a position on all parts of the legislation.
- The student used multiple evidence sources to back up opinions.
- The students provided alternative solutions where required.
- The paper was well-written, clear, concise; grammar and usage correct.

## B, Very Good
- The student took a position on most parts of the legislation.
- The student used more than one evidence source to back up opinions.
- The student provided an alternative solution where required.
- The paper was well-written, clear; grammar and usage may contain minor errors.

## C, Satisfactory
- The student took a position on some parts of the legislation.
- The student used at least one evidence source to back up opinions.
- The student provided some idea of a compromise solution where required.
- The paper was understandable; grammar and usage may contain errors.

## D, Needs Improvement
- The student took a position on a part of the legislation.
- The student used no evidence sources to back up opinions.
- The student provided no alternative solution where required.
- The paper was poorly written; grammar and usage contain major errors.

# More Than Two Political Parties?

*with Erik Walker, James Madison University*

## NCSS Theme
### Civic Ideals and Practices

"Locate, access, analyze, organize, synthesize, evaluate, and apply information about selected public issues—identifying, describing, and evaluating multiple points of view."[a]

## Objectives
### Subject Area National Standards

Civics and Government

"How does the American political system provide for choice and opportunities for participation?"[b]

"Political parties, campaigns and elections. Students should be able to evaluate, take and defend positions about the roles of political parties, campaigns and elections in American politics."[c]

### Skills Standards or Objectives

Evaluate the role of third parties in the United States.

Explain the major characteristics of American political parties, how they vary by locality, and how they reflect the dispersion of power, providing citizens numerous opportunities for participation.

### Attitude Standard or Objective

Students will appreciate that the American political system provides opportunities to citizens to express their beliefs about issues of concern.

[a] *Expectations of Excellence, p. 139*
[b] *National Standards for Civics and Government, p. 103*
[c] *p. 105*

## Procedures
### Set

- Have students brainstorm the names of the political parties that they know. Call on students for names of parties and place the names on the chalkboard. Generally, the students will know the two major parties and might be able to name a third (e.g., the Reform party).
- Ask: Do these names represent all the political options available to the citizens of the U.S.? Are there other parties?
- If you are in a computer laboratory setting, have students go to: 3rd Party Central: http://www.3pc.net/index.html

- They can then click on "Party Matchmaking Service: http://www. 3pc. net/matchmaker/index.html
- Students can take the "quiz" by selecting their beliefs about the issues listed and hitting "submit."
- A match to several third parties should appear with percentages of agreement on issues.

## *Body of Lesson*

- Students will create and complete a graphic organizer (most likely a chart or a series of Venn diagrams) that illustrates the similarities and differences of third parties with the two major political parties.
- The teacher can differentiate instruction by deciding on the number of political parties each student (or if working in groups, each group of students) should research.
- The students must identify the:
  - Name of the party
  - Mission statement of the party
  - Major planks in the party platform
  - Degree of support by the American public
    - By membership (number of members)
    - Percentage of party members elected to office, etc.
- Remind students that as they look at the party literature, they need to select a range of third parties that represent a range of viewpoints in America.

Note: If short on time, the teacher can assign the parties for students to research ensuring a range of parties across the class. Also, to save time:

- The teacher can provide a graphic organizer (chart) of political parties and issues for the students to complete individually or in groups.
- If there is very little time, the teacher could create a chart of political parties and issues out of large chart paper and post it in the classroom.
  - Each student or pair of students could research one assigned party and fill in that section of the chart.
  - The class could then examine and discuss the completed chart as a group.
  - The chart could also be created on the teacher's computer (if available).
  - The students fill in their section, and the teacher can print out the completed chart and make copies for the students' notebooks.

## *Closure*

- Students will present their graphic organizers to the class and explain what they have learned about the major issues these party platforms represent and the degree of support they have with the American public.
- The teacher can post the graphic organizers around the room for the class to share and look at more carefully.

- The unit or chapter exam could include an essay question asking students to compare and contrast several political party beliefs on specific issues.

## Timing

The timing will vary with the teacher's resources.

- For the students who can do their research in the computer lab, the home pages for a variety of political parties are listed below. These can be supplied to the students to speed up the lesson.
- If there is no lab access, the teacher will have to download and print out the information from the Web sites and place it into individual folders. Students would use the folders during class to access the information.
- Students working in groups to create graphic organizers will take more time than if the teacher supplies an organizer—probably a chart with the issues down the left-hand column and spaces for the party names across the top. The number of parties required for this research will affect the time the lesson takes.
- Presenting the organizers to the class is time consuming.

## Materials

### General Information about Political Parties

- U.S. political parties: http://www.politics1.com/parties.htm
- 3rd Party Central: http://www.3pc.net/index.html
- Political Parties and Youth Organizations in the US: http://www.sv.uit.no/seksjon/statsvit/engver/links/polpar/usa.htm
- Political Parties online in the US: http://www.geocities.com/editorialist1/parties.htm

### Major Political Parties

- Democratic Party: http://www.democrats.org/index.html
- Republican Party: http://www.rnc.org/

### Third Parties in America

- The American Party: http://www.theamericanparty.org/
- The American Heritage Party: http://www.americanheritageparty.org/
- The American Independent Party: http://www.aipca.org/
- The American Reform Party: http://www.americanreform.org/
- The Communist Party in America: http://www.cpusa.org/
- The Constitution Party: http://www.constitutionparty.com/
- The Family Values Party: http://members.aol.com/fvparty/fvparty1/
- The Green Party: http://www.greenparties.org/
- The Vermont Grassroots Party: http://www.vermontel.com/~epgorge/vgrp.htm
- The Freedom Socialist Party: http://www.socialism.com/

- The Independence Party: http://www.eindependence.org/
- The Light Party: http://www.lightparty.com/index.shtml
- Natural Law Party: http://www.natural-law.org/
- The New Party: http://www.newparty.org/
- The New Union Party: http://www1.minn.net/~nup/
- The Peace and Freedom Party: http://www.peaceandfreedom.org/
- The Prohibition Party: http://www.prohibition.org/
- The Reform Party: http://www.reformparty.org/
- The Revolution Party: http://www.revolting.com/
- Socialist Party USA: http://www.sp-usa.org/
- Socialist Action Party: http://www.socialistaction.org/
- The Socialist Equality Party: http://www.wsws.org/sections/category/icfi/sepuscat.shtml
- The Socialist Labor Party: http://www.slp.org/
- The Southern Party: http://www.southernparty.org/
- The United States Pacifist Party: http://www.geocities.com/CapitolHill/Lobby/4826/
- We the People Party: http://www.wethepeople-wtp.org/
- The World Workers Party: http://www.workers.org/

**Additional Parties Not Yet Fielding Candidates for Office**
- The American Liberty Party: http://www.americanlibertyparty.homestead.com/
- America's Party: http://www.ap2000.addr.com/
- The Constitutionalist Party: http://home.earthlink.net/~jmarkels/cp.html
- Libertarian National Socialist Green Party: http://www.nazi.org/
- Constitutional Action Party: http://www2.ari.net/home/CAP/
- The Multicapitalist Party: http://www.oicu2.com/afc/
- Revolutionary Communist Party USA: http://www.rwor.org/rcp-e.html
- The 3rd Party of America: http://www.3rdparty.org/
- The Progressive Labor Party: http://www.plp.org/
- Democratic Socialists of America: http://www.dsausa.org/index.html

# Evaluation Rubric

| | Excellent | Very Good | Satisfactory | Needs Improvement |
|---|---|---|---|---|
| Names of third party | Used three or more third parties; third parties cover a range of beliefs | Used two or more third parties; parties chosen differ in beliefs | Used one third party; little or no difference between party chosen and two major parties | Did not select a valid third party |
| Mission of party | Clearly, concisely outlined party mission | Understands mission of the party and explains well | Has a basic idea of party mission | Does not understand party mission |
| Major party platform planks | Lists all major party issues for all parties discussed | Lists most issues for all parties or all issues for fewer parties | Lists of issues are incomplete or there are errors | Has little or no understanding of party issues |
| Degree of support by American public | Lists both membership and percent of candidates elected for each party; information is correct | Lists either membership or percent of candidates elected for each party | Does not list degree of support or membership for third parties but does for two major parties; may have errors | Degree of support not indicated, or major errors |
| Compared with the two major parties | Compared each party with the two major parties | Compared most parties with the two major parties | Compared at least one third party with the two major parties | Did not include a third party; may not have compared two major parties |
| Contrasted with the two major parties | Contrasted each party with the two major parties | Contrasted most parties with the two major parties | Contrasted at least one third party with the two major parties | Did not include a third party; may not have contrasted two major parties |

| Graphic organizer | Clearly labeled the parties; easy to read and distinguish different groups; thorough in displaying information available | Clearly labeled the parties; easy to read; may have minor errors; was unable to display all information available | Labeled the parties; errors; minimum information displayed | Confusing; parties not clearly marked; major errors; little to no information displayed |
|---|---|---|---|---|

# Conclusion

Now that you have had an opportunity to review the lessons in this book, I hope you will feel free to mix and match the instructional strategies and the rubrics as best fits your individual curriculum and student needs. The lesson rubrics have been designed to include differing examples for differing student achievement levels and instructional strategies. Although it is true that most of the lessons have a requirement that includes a written paper of some sort, it is entirely appropriate to modify the performance outcomes of the lessons to include role playing, simulations, a poster or other artistic creation. Just keep in mind that elaborated conversation reflecting a depth of understanding is one of the keys to successful authentic assessment. Then design a rubric to take that factor into account.

With the lessons in this book as a starting point, I wish you success in modifying your instruction to reflect authentic learning. The basic principles of authentic learning (instruction and assessment combined) discussed in this book included: higher-order thinking; depth of knowledge; connectedness to the world beyond the classroom; substantive conversation; and social support for student achievement. The implementation of these principles into your instruction should ensure increased retention with a focus on true understanding and meaning. Good luck!

# References

ASCD. (1992, May). Using performance assessment. *Educational Leadership, 49*(8).

ASCD. (1996–1997, December–January). Teaching for authentic student performance. *Educational Leadership, 54*(4).

ASCD. (1999, March). Using standards and assessment. *Educational Leadership, 56*(6).

Bloom, B. S. (Ed.). (1984) *Taxonomy of educational objective: The classification of educational goals.* New York: Longman.

Bruner, J. S. (1960). *The process of education.* Cambridge, MA: Harvard University Press.

Burz, H. L., & Marshall, K. (1998). *Performance-based curriculum for social studies: From knowing to showing.* CA: Corwin Press.

Center for Civic Education. (1994). *National standards for civics and government.*

Cohen, P. (1995, August). Designing performance assessment tasks. *Education Update, 37*(6), 1, 4–5, 8.

Cornett, J. W. (1993, Summer). Authentic assessment and thoughtful social studies teaching and learning. *Trends and Issues,* 5–8.

Cronin, J. F. (1993, April). Four misconceptions about authentic learning. *Educational Leadership, 50*(7), 78–80.

Engle, S. H., & Ochoa, A. S. (1988). *Education for democratic citizenship: Decision making in the social studies.* New York: Teachers College Press.

Elliott, S. N. (1998). Performance assessment of students' achievement: Research and practice. *Learning Disabilities Research and Practice, 13*(4), 233–241.

Erickson, H. L. (1998). *Concept-based curriculum and instruction: Teaching beyond the facts.* Thousand Oaks, CA: Corwin Press.

Evans, R. W., & Saxe, D. W. (Eds.). (1996). *Handbook on teaching social issues.* Washington, D.C.: NCSS.

Gardner, H. (1999) *The disciplined mind: What all students should understand.* New York: Simon & Schuster.

Gardner, H. (1983). *Frames of mind: The theory of multiple intelligence.* New York: Basic Books.

Geography Education Standards Project. (1994). *Geography for life: What every young American should know and be able to do in geography.*

George, P. S., McEwin, C. K., & Jenkins, J. M. (2000). *The exemplary high school.* Fort Worth, TX: Harcourt College Publications.

Gordon, R. (1998, January). Balancing real-world problems with real-world result. *Phi Delta Kappan, 79*(5), 390–393.

Gordon, R. (1998, March). A curriculum for authentic learning. *The Education Digest, 63*(7), 4–8.

Harrington, D., et al. (1994). Authentic teaching and assessment: Policy and practice, examples from the field. National Center for Restructuring Education, Schools, and Teaching Affiliates Annual Meeting, New York. (ERIC Document Reproduction Service No. ED374095)

Hess, F. M. (1999). *Bringing the social sciences alive.* Boston: Allyn and Bacon.

International Society for Technology in Education. (2000). *National education technology standards for students: Connecting curriculum and technology.*

Ivey, O. T., & Hickson, M. (1974). *A basic approach to social studies: An overview for teachers and parents.* (Eric Document Reproduction Service No. ED160517)

Korbin, D. (1996). *Beyond the textbook: Teaching history using documents and primary sources.* Portsmouth, NH: Heinemann.

Lewin, L., & Shoemaker, B. J. (1998). *Great performances: Creating classroom-based assessment tasks.* Alexandria, VA: ASCD.

Maksimowicz, M. L. (1993). *Focus on authentic learning and assessment in the middle school.* (ERIC Document Reproduction Service No. ED380226)

Martorella, P. H. (1997). Technology and social studies. *Theory and Research in Social Education 25*(4), 511–514.

Massialas, B. G., & Allen, R. F. (1996). *Critical issues in teaching social studies K–12.* Belmont, CA: Wadsworth Publishing.

Means, B., & Olson, K. (1994, April). The link bewteen technology and authentic learning. *Educational Leadership, 51*(7), 15–18.

Nagel, N. G. (1993). *Authentic learning/authentic assessment: Let's begin with tomorrow's teachers.* (ERIC Document Reproduction No. ED412184)

National Center for History in the Schools. (1994). *National standards for world history: Exploring paths to the present.* Los Angeles: .

National Center for History in the Schools. (1996). *National standards for history, basic edition.* Los Angeles: .

National Council for the Social Studies. (1994). *Expectations of excellence: Curriculum standards for social studies.* Washington, D.C.

National Council on Economic Education. (1998). *Voluntary national content standards in economics.* New York, NY.

Newmann, F. M. (1984) *Social studies in U.S. schools: Mainstream practice and radical potential.* (ERIC Document Reproduction Service No. ED247166)

Newmann, F. M. (1987). *Citizenship education in the United States: A statement of needs.* (ERIC Document Reproduction Service No. ED307203)

Newmann, F. M. (1988, January). Can depth replace coverage in the high school curriculum. *Phi Delta Kappan, 69,* 345–348.

Newmann, F. M. (1989, October). Reflective civic participation. *Social Education, 53*(6), 357–366.

Newmann, F. M. (1991). Linking restructuring to authentic student achievement. *Phi Delta Kappan.* (ERIC Document Reproduction Service No. ED384472)

Newmann, F. M. (1997). Authentic assessment in social studies: Standards and examples. In *Handbook of Classroom Assessment* (pp. 359–380). Academic Press.

Newmann, F. M., & Associates. (1996a). *Authentic achievement: Restructuring schools for intellectual quality.* San Francisco: Jossey-Bass.

Newmann, F. M., et al. (1995a, April). *Authentic pedagogy and student performance.* Paper presented at the Annual Meeting of the American Educational Research Association, San Francisco. (ERIC Document Reproduction Service No. ED389679)

Newmann, F. M., et al. (1995b). Authentic pedagogy: Standards that boost student performance. *Issues in Restructuring Schools* (Issue Report No. 8). Center on Organization and Restructuring of Schools. (ERIC Document Reproduction Service No: ED390906)

Newmann, F. M., et al. (1996b). Authentic pedagogy and student performance. *American Journal of Education, 104*(4), 280–312.

Newmann, F. M., Marks, H. M., & Gamorman, A. (1995, April 18–22). *Authentic pedagogy and student performance.* Paper presented at the annual meeting of the American Educational Research Association, San Francisco. (ERIC Document Reproduction Service No. ED389679)

Newmann, F. M., & Oliver, D. W. (1970). *Clarifying public controversy: An approach to teaching social studies.* Boston: Little, Brown.

Newmann, F. M., & Wehlage, G. G. (1993). Five standards of authentic instruction. *Educational Leadership, 50*(7), 8–12.

Nickell, P. (1993). Alternative assessment: Implications for social studies. *ERIC Digest.* (ERIC Document Reproduction Service No. ED360219)

Nickell, P. (Ed.). (1999, October). Authentic assessment in social studies. *Social Education, 63*(6).

Northwest Regional Educational Laboratory. (1997). *Bibliography of assessment alternatives: Social studies.* Portland, OR: Assessment Resource Library, Evaluation and Assessment Program.

Oliver, D. W., & Newmann, F. M. (1970). *Clarifying public controversy: An approach to teaching social studies.* Boston: Little, Brown.

Owings, A. (1995). *Frauen: German women recall the third reich.* NJ: Rutgers University Press.

Parker, W. C. (1991). *Renewing the social studies curriculum.* Alexandria, VA: ASCD.

Passe, J. (1996). *When students chose content: A guide to increasing motivation, autonomy, and achievement.* CA: Corwin Press.

Perkins, D. (1994, February 4–7). Putting understanding upfront. *Educational Leadership.*

Phi Delta Kappa (1999, May). Special section on performance assessment. *Kappan, 80*(9), 658–695.

Popham, W. J. (1999). *Classroom assessment: What teachers need to know* (2nd ed.). Boston: Allyn and Bacon.

Prentice Hall. *Cooperative Learning Project: Evaluation form A: Process* http://www.phschool.com/professional_development/assessment/rub_coop_process.cfm

*Random House dictionary of the English language* (2nd ed.). (1987). New York: Random House.

Riley, K. L., & Stern, B. S. (1997a, November 22). *Teaching difficult concepts through authentic assessment.* Paper presented at the Annual Meeting of the National Council of the Social Studies, Cincinnati, OH.

Riley, K.L and Stern, B.S. (1997b). *Curriculum, teaching and authentic assessment: Using qualitative methodology to bridge theory into practice.* (ERIC Document Reproduction Service No. ED434041)

Riley, K. L., & Stern, B. S. (1998). Classroom challenges in schools of education: Using authentic assessment and qualitative methodology to bridge theory into practice. *The Educational Forum, 61,* 2.

Riley, K. L., Wilson, E. K., & Fogg, T. (2000). Transforming the spirit of teaching through wise practice: Observations of two Alabama social studies teachers. *Social Education, 64*(6), 361–363.

Scheurman, G., & Newmann, F. M. (1998, January). Authentic intellectual work in social studies: Putting performance before pedagogy. *Social Education, 62*(1), 23–25

Secretary's Commission on Achieving Necessary Skills (SCANS). (1991). *What work requires of schools.* http://www.academicinnovations.com/report.html

Sherry, L. (1997). *Linking technology with promising practices to improve teaching and learning.* (ERIC Document Reproduction Services No. ED414277)

Solomon, P.G. (1998). *The curriculum bridge: From standards to actual classroom practice.* CA: Corwin Press.

Stern, B. S. (1995, November 10). *Restructuring high school social studies: Problem solving, critical thinking and technology.* Paper presented at the annual meeting of the National Council of the Social Studies, Chicago.

Stern, B. S. (1998a, November 19). Adios to tears: Teaching historical empathy using first person accounts. In *Historical empathy and the wartime internment of enemy aliens: Theory into practice.* Symposium conducted at the annual meeting of the College and University Faculty Assembly of the National Council for the Social Studies.

Stern, B. S. (1998b). Addressing the concept of historical empathy: Frauen, German women recall the third reich. *International Journal on Social Education, 13*(1) 43–48.

Stern, B. S. (2000a). Authentic learning and foundations of education: A naturalistic inquiry of past learning experiences. *Teaching and Curriculum Dialogue, 2*(1),12–19.

Stern, B. S. (2000b, November 30). *Authentic learning and social studies.* Session presented to the Virginia Association for Supervision and Curriculum Development, Williamsburg, VA.

Stern, B. S. (2000c). *Teaching primary sources with historical empathy.* Presented to the James Madison University Center for School Leadership Summer Secondary Social Studies SOL Content Academy.

Stern, B. S. (2000d). *Theories of urban place location* (interactive PowerPoint session). Presented to the James Madison University Center for School Leadership Summer Secondary Social Studies SOL Content Academy.

Stern, B. S. (2000e, October 20). *Using primary sources to develop understanding.* Session presented at the annual conference of the Virginia Social Studies Educators, Norfolk, VA.

Stern, B. S., & Riley, K. L. (1999, November). *Teaching about social issues.* Session presented at the annual meeting of the National Council for the Social Studies, Orlando, FL.

Stern, B. S., & Riley, K. L. (2000, November 17). *Authentic instruction: Integrating technology into social studies.* Multimedia session presented at the annual meeting of the National Council for the Social Studies, San Antonio, TX.

Thornton, S. J. (1998). *The persistent problem of method in social studies teaching.* (Eric Document Reproduction Service No. ED427987)

Thornton, S. J. (1989). *Aspiration and practice: Teacher as curricular-instructional gatekeeper in social studies.* (Eric Document Reproduction Service No. ED315347)

Todorov, K. R., & Brousseau, B. (1997). *Social studies authentic assessment project.* Lansing, MI: Michigan Department of Education.

United States Department of Labor, Secretary's Commission on Achieving Necessary Skills. (1992). Learning a living: A blueprint for high performance: A SCANS report for America 2000. Washington, DC: Author.

Wiggins, G. (1990). The case for authentic assessment. *ERIC Digest.* (ERIC Document Reproduction Service No. ED328611)

Wiggins, G. (1996). Practicing what we preach in designing authentic assessments. *Educational Leadership, 54*(4), 18–25.

Wiggins, G. (1998). *Educative assessment: Designing assessments to inform and improve student performance.* San Francisco: Jossey-Bass.

Wiggins, G. (1999). *Understanding by design.* Session presented at the annual meeting of the Virginia ASCD, Williamsburg, VA.

Wiske, M. S. (1994, February). How teaching for understanding changes the rules in the classroom. *Educational Leadership, 51*(5),19–21.

Yeager, E. A. (2000). Thoughts on wise practice in the teaching of social studies. *Social Education, 64*(6), 352–353.

Zmuda, A., & Tomaino, M. (2001). *The competent classroom: Aligning high school curriculum, standards and assessment—A creative teaching guide.* New York: Teachers College Press.